Surviving Divorce

Daily Affirmations

Sefra Kobrin Pitzele

Health Communications, Inc.
Deerfield Beach, Florida

© 1991 Sefra Kobrin Pitzele

ISBN 1-55874-118-6

Publisher: Health Communications, Inc.
3201 S.W. 15th Street
Deerfield Beach, Florida 33442-8190

Cover design by Iris T. Slones

For a long while I have wanted to write a book to help people deal with the difficult problems that can arise during a divorce. Naturally, I had to wait for the passage of time and personal healing from my own divorce. Then, I began to cast about to find the right format. One evening when my son Mark was home from college for a visit, he suggested I write a book of affirmations on separation and divorce, similar to my second book, *One More Day.* I thought about his suggestion for a week or two, and realized he was absolutely right.

A book of positive affirmations, one that addresses the problems we all have had dealing with failing relationships, separation and divorce, was just the format I had been looking for. And so to Mark David Pitzele, for helping me decide how to present this information, I give extra special thanks and I dedicate this book, *Surviving Divorce.*

Very special people offer us support during our most trying times. My two daughters, Debbi and Amy, as well as Mark, are always there to encourage me and to offer their help in a most unselfish way. To my close friends I offer love and thanks, for always being available to give hugs and emotional support, and for all the times we laugh and cry together. And a very special thank you to Ruth E. Powers, who helped convince me I should begin writing.

And most especially, for their time, their caring and their friendship, I offer my deepest gratitude to Rabbi Julie Gordon and Rabbi Jonathon Ginsburg. Their patience, time, compassion and understanding has taught me a very special, new, and personal understanding for the title of Rabbi.

To the Reader

There are no two ways about it, breaking up with someone we once pledged our undying love to is very hard. We were under the impression we'd stay married "until death do us part." We were wrong. Regardless of how difficult the relationship was at the end of our marriage, some small part of us mourns the love that was there in the beginning. Also, we may chastise ourselves for our role in the divorce, even if we were relatively blameless.

Single again, perhaps dealing with children and quite often an altered financial picture, we have all kinds of new adjustments to make.

Surviving Divorce is a gentle affirmation book designed to show the universality of relationships and marriage problems. It talks about the difficulties we faced during marriage and some ways we can work to solve them, as well as the relief of being out of what may have been an uncertain, unloving and perhaps abusive relationship.

Most importantly, *Surviving Divorce* affirms each one of us as a valuable human being, a good person. We are single again, some by choice and others through no fault of our own. We are getting stronger emotionally and are moving toward the excitement and the joys of life on our own. Whether we choose to remain single or decide to marry again some day, we are all entitled to live the most wonderful lives possible. I pray we will be happy with whatever decision we make since we are all entitled to peaceful, happy and contented lives.

Please drop me a postcard at P.O. Box 16294, St. Paul, MN 55116, with brief ideas that have not been discussed in this book. I'll begin a file for the next one!

Sefra Kobrin Pitzele

Sefra Kobrin Pitzele is the author of two previous books, *We Are Not Alone: Learning to Live with Chronic Illness* (Workman 1986) and *One More Day: Daily Meditations for the Chronically Ill* (Hazelden/Harper 1988). Having finished *Surviving Divorce,* Sefra is already hard at work on another book.

Frequently invited to give keynote speeches and conduct workshops, largely about dealing with chronic illness, she accepts both national and local speaking invitations as often as her systemic lupus erythematosus and Sjogren's syndrome, the two connective tissue diseases she has, allow.

Besides writing and giving speeches, Ms. Pitzele also serves as a co-founder and co-publisher of *ADVANTAGE: A Magazine for People with Chronic Health Conditions,* (non-profit, Minnesota). She serves as Secretary of the National Sjogren's Syndrome Association and a board member of the NSSA/Twin Cities/MN Chapter and is on the Operations Committee of the Minnesota Chapter of the Lupus Foundation of America.

Sefra Kobrin Pitzele lives in St. Paul, Minnesota with her daughter Amy, a senior in high school. Her other two children, Debbi and Mark, are adults and live on their own.

We never forget a person we have loved. We may remember the day, what time it was and even what we were wearing when we first felt that love. Years later we can conjure up the warm and exciting feelings we had.

At the time we decided to marry, we never dreamed our love would end unhappily. So yet another memory is added — the day we decided to part. For a while we try to forget our time together. We deny we miss the very person we just divorced.

As time passes we recognize that forgetting is an impossible task. We will remember and, hopefully, be able to separate the good times from the bad.

. . . .

While I cannot forget my past love,
in time the memories will become
bittersweet. I am working hard
to make that happen.

No One Is Perfect

"I could handle that child better than that," one neighbor intones. "She's never been any good at relationships," says another. "I remember when their parents screamed at each other all hours of the night." We've all made such catty remarks, most often secretly, never really intending that anyone hear us.

Each one of us at some time feels we can do it better, that we can succeed where others have failed. But when push comes to shove, we suffer, too, from a failing relationship, from lack of success on the job or with children who misbehave.

We would like to pretend we're perfect, that no one does it as well as we do but with maturity we understand that life is made of successes and failures.

. . . .

I try hard to live as good a life as I can.
No one can expect any more than that.

Too many of us have a tendency to chastise ourselves about all we may have done wrong during our marriage. "If only I hadn't been an enabler," we lament. Or, "It would have been different if I'd just had a better job."

Finally, after many months or even years of attending support groups, we deem ourselves ready to enter the mainstream of dating once again. We feel open, willing to try once more, to take the first step, to open up to love. As we do, we may be surprised to find that our old wounds are not totally healed and that growth and change are both very long processes.

. . . .

Even while I work my program,
I can let myself be open to new
and exciting friendships.

3

One of us eventually has to leave the house or the apartment. As clothes are packed and knicknacks, tools and books are put into boxes, pieces of memories seem to be stuffed into the suitcase along with them — memories of how well we used to dance together, how much fun we had on that first vacation or how we held each other and laughed and cried with joy when the baby was born.

There is no easy way to leave. Endings can be so painful, especially if there are children involved. We don't know how we will manage or if we will be able to manage at all. We wonder if we will survive.

As the weeks and months go by, we begin to find our new style of living and we recognize that we can go on, day by day, until we become whole again.

. . . .

Although this is hard to remember all the time, I still have my dignity.

Most of us would agree that constantly feeling sorry for oneself is not fruitful. However, after a relationship has split up — temporarily or permanently — we begin to grieve as surely as if a loved one had died. The love we felt really did "die." Surprised at the intensity of our feelings, we worry about future relationships.

We grieve even after the end of an unstable, unhappy marriage. We grieve for what might have been. There is a void in our lives — an empty place where a person and a whole pattern of living used to be.

Mourning a lost love is perfectly normal and we can take solace in knowing that others grieve as well.

. . . .

While I cannot rush the grieving process,
I can stay aware of what is happening
to me and why, and know that
my feelings are normal.

The thought of dating again looms large before us. Few of us want to live the rest of our lives alone so we have to face the "singles scene." Where do we begin? How do we find other interesting single people? We form a plan.

Some decide to meet people by joining special interest groups, such as Parents Without Partners, taking a class or attending Alcoholics Anonymous (AA) or Adult Children of Alcoholics (ACoA) meetings. Others meet new friends at churches, synagogues or lectures.

First encounters are hard but we realize that others have been divorced, too, and that they are also looking for new friends. We find that there are a lot of lonely people, many of whom felt as unsure and as alone as we did about beginning again.

. . . .

My first attempts at meeting others of
the opposite sex are difficult but this
is important to me. I will continue
to keep myself involved with
groups and community activities.

When we first fell in love, in our eyes, our chosen spouse could do no wrong. The first several months or years may even have been idyllic. Then we began to notice certain problems that annoyed us. Perhaps it was the household chores left undone or a financial issue.

It is hard to know when the uncertainty began — the nagging feeling that things just weren't going well. Now that the marriage has dissolved, now that we are living separate lives, we can begin to see that neither of us was wholly to blame. Perhaps our family of origin had problems that we carried into our adult life or our expectations, behaviors and basic personality structures did not match.

I will not blame myself solely for a failed relationship. I am working hard to identify my weak areas so I will not fail again.

There was a joke we used to tell as children about a man who had a flea circus. When he held open his palm to show off his tiny performers, he seemed delighted. Then he forgot and accidentally applauded at his own cleverness, smashing his flea circus as he clapped his hands.

Feeling frightened is common in fearful situations. The very first step is admitting our fear and getting ready to begin again. In reaching out to make contact with other people — people who are willing to care about us, to enter into our lives, to share our problems — we must remember to hold our palms open, to reach out to others. With palms open, arms reaching out, we know we are getting ready to trust again.

. . . .

It has been hard for me to make
emotional contact with another person.
Today I am willing to let
myself begin to trust.

One man was always making excuses for his wife's behavior, for her temper, for her foul language and even for the times when she hit the children. "What reason do you have to stay with her, John?" his friends and family would ask over and over again.

"Well, I love her. And besides, I believe in our marriage vows. She doesn't really mean to act that way," he would answer. "In between episodes," he told his family, "she's wonderful." One fateful day her temper resulted in a broken arm for their nine-year-old.

John realized that by not protesting his wife's behavior he was, in fact, sanctioning it. He told her he was leaving if she didn't change and they decided to start therapy together — designed to help her find out why she behaved that way and to help him understand why he tolerated the behavior.

. . . .

I am responsible for what I do.
From today on I will own my behavior.

Blooming

The papers are signed. Divorced. So final. Like a door slamming shut in our faces. Now what, we wonder. One thing is sure, few of us are purposely willing to make the same mistakes over again. And so we begin the search to find some answers about ourselves.

Breaking old habits is no easy job but that's just what we have to do to keep from being co-dependent in our next relationship. Working a program, step by step, is slow and very, very hard work. In order to recover we must learn to trust enough to break all our ingrained family rules. We learn to tell the truth. We learn to talk about feelings. Slowly, we move from one step to another and slowly, we begin to bloom.

*I have enough faith in myself now
to move forward with my
own new personal rules.*

It is often a common theme that before a marriage really ends there are several false stops and starts. "I'm gonna leave you!" one partner threatens, while the other one snarls, "Go right ahead. I don't need you!"

And then someone cries, apologies are made, perhaps flowers are purchased and we kiss and make up. Over and over we repeat the same behavior. For a while things go smoothly. We both make a supreme and very uncomfortable effort to keep the quiet times going.

Eventually we recognize that there is just no joy left in making up and we know that a marriage isn't meant to be conducted on eggshells. It is truly over. In order to move on, we need to understand why the marriage failed and what part we had in its failure.

. . . .

I can say farewell to a marriage
that is finished without giving up
on myself. I am worth saving.

Family Rules

In most dysfunctional families there are dozens of rules, many of which are not mentioned. Family members know the rules, the most important of which is never to talk about family problems with anyone.

Breaking family rules can cause major difficulties. We adopt our own way to function best within that framework. Some survive being the silent ones — the good ones — the ones who never ripple the water. The good ones work hard in school, never pick a fight and are often very quiet. Others are caregivers or they misbehave.

We take our childhood behaviors and roles with us right into adulthood, right into our adult relationships. It is no surprise that we feel responsible for all the problems that occur in our families.

. . . .

*Today marks the start of my right
to take risks, to make myself heard,
to express my opinions. I do not
always have to be "good."
I can learn to be myself.*

Many of us enter into adult life fully aware of the failures and difficulties of our parents behind us. We resolve not to make the same mistakes.

We may go into debt from overspending or gambling or from using drugs. By denying the problem, we continue our out-of-control behavior until our loved ones stage a confrontation and we have to face it.

Recovery is not easy. We agonize while we try to work through a lifetime of habits. If we want it badly enough, if we have emotional support from friends and family and if we stick with our program, we can feel the pride that comes with positive change.

I know my Higher Power forgives all but first I must continue my steps to forgive myself.

"I've never met anyone who makes me feel like this." During courtship there were a few things that made her feel uncomfortable but she remained convinced that after marriage things would change.

When asked what she was concerned about, she answered that he had a bit of a temper and had slapped her across the face a couple of times. Yet he was always contrite, gentle and very loving for days after each episode.

But things got worse. After years of abuse she went to a counselor, frightened for her life. The social worker helped her leave him and move immediately into a shelter for battered women. Once she learned to place the focus upon herself, to look after her own needs, there was no turning back.

. . . .

No one deserves to be abused. By moving out I have taken my first step.

As younger people, we carry around a mental picture of our ideal mate. "I want to marry a well-built blond with a dazzling smile." A friend counters with, "Not me. I'm into sports. Mine has to be a jogger. I'd never marry a couch potato!"

When we meet the man or woman of our dreams, our former ideas disappear. First, it's usually a case of chemistry. Our emotional and physical fire is lit and we can think of no one else as a potential spouse.

When the fire becomes an ember and a real relationship takes over, too few of us are willing to work through the ups and downs to make a marriage work. The lucky ones who work hard at a relationship find themselves more in love as times goes on.

. . . .

May our love continue to grow
and may we never lose sight of our
commitment to each other.

Bells ring. People who pass by smile at us. We are truly in love. But one day the bells don't ring as loudly and not every day is glorious. Some of the high-intensity wonder begins to fade. The exciting and often sexual beginnings of marriage move over as reality settles in. Bills, not bells, often take precedence.

Conflicts begin and are not always resolved. Behaviors annoy us and we complain. Underwear gets left on the floor and toothpaste gets squeezed wrong. At this time many recognize the marriage is in crisis. How the problems are handled usually determines the course of the rest of the marriage.

. . . .

My marriage means a great deal to me
and I will put forth the same effort
to save it as I did to create it.

How our family functioned, what behaviors our parents demonstrated — positive or not — all influenced our adult behavior. We tend to carry with us all the interactions and roles we learned during childhood.

With loving and supportive parents, many of us came from highly functional homes. We learned to love from parents who gave us unqualified love, who cared deeply and showed us affection. We developed strong friendships and were encouraged to express our feelings.

As adults we know what kind of home we came from. We remember our childhood with increasing clarity. Those who came from functional families usually became functional adults. Those who did not can get help.

. . . .

My family can function as a close and supportive family unit as long as we love and support one another.

Another Crisis

As we grow up and leave our parents' home, many of us choose to get married. Moving out of young adulthood and into our 30s, we work hard to create a good life together. Children add yet another dimension. We change addresses, finish school or vocational training, buy houses and change jobs, until finally we begin to feel settled and content.

Why, then, do so many of us still go through a midlife crisis? Why do we reach a personal point of no return and feel compelled to either change professions, our way of life or possibly our marriage partners?

Even though it may mean hurting others, often people whom we love, we cannot always deny what we need to do for ourselves. We must take care of ourselves.

. . . .

My needs and feelings have to be acknowledged and allowed. I only hope that I can grow without hurting the ones I love.

The final words ring in our ears and cause our eyes to suddenly sting. "It's over. We just can't go on like this." Our marriage is done — no more will we have to struggle with a relationship that has grown stifling and uncomfortable.

So why do we still cry when the disk jockey plays "our song?" We are amazed at how quickly human nature causes us to forget the problems and only remember the gentler moments.

We may cry, we certainly will grieve over even an unsuccessful marriage, yet somehow we come out whole enough to begin again at the other end. And we surprise ourselves with the strength we never knew we had.

The gift of potential new relationships will be ready when I am ready.

Puppy love. Oh my, how we yearned for that first kiss. Passing notes in class, hanging like suction cups near the telephone! School dances, sodas and Saturday movies filled our time together. And then it ended. Puppy love.

Reasons for the breakup ranged from the ridiculous to the sublime. "I hated her braces" or "He was a nerd." And then we fell in love again. This time harder. This time longer.

With maturity we added depth and breadth to our relationships. A very special person came along and we fell in love, this time seriously. We learned to give and take, to compromise with our loved one, for this was the relationship that was going to last us a lifetime.

By allowing myself to remember young love, I can grow in today's relationship.

One person is fired and responds, "Well, wonderful opportunities could be just around the corner." His colleague, also asked to leave, falls into depression and a long series of "what ifs."

There were serious problems in our marriage, yet we may still be surprised when it ends. Rather than finding out what was wrong, we may prefer to savor the bitterness we feel at our estranged spouse. We could spend our days asking "what if?" Or we could decide to correct our problems and get on with our lives.

By giving ourselves permission to move forward, to grow personally, we can begin to trust again, both ourselves and a new love. Many wonderful people are willing to help us function successfully again.

Let me not be so blinded by my anger that I fail to recognize that the breakup of my marriage has not ended my life.

It seems as if our lives are falling apart. Our coveted job isn't working out. The car is a lemon and the roof needs to be replaced. Even our kids aren't perfect. Worst of all, the person we've loved all these years seems to be changing before our very eyes and we just don't understand.

Griping and groaning about all the changes going on, we wonder if a midlife crisis is creeping up on us. We finally comprehend that we, too, have been changing.

Only when we have opened our minds to the possibility that we have problems, too, do we give ourselves the right to recover, to change our difficult behaviors. And then we can get on with our lives.

. . . .

Today marks the beginning of my
willingness to get help, to recognize
that I have the ability and desire
to change my behavior.
I have not been blameless.

Carl had been seeing a therapist for many weeks. One afternoon she said, "Tell me what you're really thinking about right now. Share with me your true feelings about your father." Carl was taken aback. "I am. I'm telling the truth about him."

"But Carl, you're sharing some bitter and painful childhood memories with me. Why are you smiling?" Carl said he didn't know why he was smiling.

Matching his face and feelings wasn't easy since he often felt quite vulnerable. Carl learned, in time, to trust himself to take personal risks, to expose his innermost emotions. It was okay to cry when he felt sad. By allowing himself to show his true feelings, Carl was well on the path to personal recovery.

. . . .

My face can match my feelings,
even when I am not happy. It is
okay for me to not smile.

Little Lies

Just a tiny white lie. We all do it. Call in to work sick when we really aren't. Tell the boss we love his tie while in truth, we feel it's exceeded in ugliness only by the local garbage dump.

In some cases it escalates before we realize what has happened. Charles comes home late, night after night, once with a blond hair on his lapel. "My barber is a lady. She has blond hair," he says glibly. June swears she doesn't drink, when it is quite apparent that she does. Doubts creep in as we lose faith in one another.

Small lies gain momentum as if they were snowballs rolling downhill. We have a hard time separating the truth from the untruths and we have learned to lie to the one we love. If the lying doesn't end, the marriage will.

. . . .

I tell small lies too often.
From now on I will be more
honest with the ones I love.

"You're better off without him," our friends exclaim. "Your marriage wasn't any good. She had a really erratic personality."

We recoil when people we thought cared about us make such unkind yet allegedly heartfelt comments. We know it's over. What friends don't know is how hurt we are by their comments and how much we miss our marriage partner. A large gap has been left in our lives, even if we couldn't stay together By criticizing our ex-partner, they criticize us for ever having chosen that person in the first place.

For a long time our spouse was our best friend, our confidant, our lover, the one with whom we shared years of memories. Being divorced doesn't mean we won't miss the person we once deeply loved.

. . . .

I understand my friends' good
intentions and will not be hurt at how
they attempt to comfort me.

Too often marriages stay together just because of the children. If these children were
asked, as adults, whether they had wished for a
divorce, many would answer yes — that they
had hated the yelling, hated the bickering.

Children always know when parents aren't
happy. Some have school problems; others revert to childish behaviors such as bedwetting,
thumbsucking or whining. They get headaches
and stomachaches.

It's a difficult decision to leave a marriage but
even harder when there are children involved.
Some of the joys and, of course, the sorrows as
well, are missed by the parent who moves out.
Leaving children is one of the most heart-
wrenching aspects of a divorce.

. . . .

I am divorcing my spouse, not my children.
I vow never to leave my children.

We worry about strange things when our marriage ends. Some are concerned about finances, others fret over the loss of their best friend. One woman wondered who she would be buried next to when she died.

For so many years we have been part of a twosome, part of the world of couples — someone's husband, someone's wife. Now, all of a sudden, we have to face the world as a single person again.

Starting over is never easy. But doing it as a divorcee takes thought and planning. How do we begin? Where do we go to meet other singles? Spreading the word among friends that we are ready can help. Attending meetings, concerts and classes where other people in similar circumstances might be, is a good way. We cope as well as we can.

. . . .

It is scary for me to begin dating again
but I will not let my insecurity keep
me from finding new friends.

We expect our marriage to last. Our union becomes complete as we share more than just physical feelings. We share successes, disappointments, changes in jobs and health.

Looking through a family album, we recall the circumstances surrounding each picture. "Remember? That was about two hours before Joanne fell off her first two-wheeler. She had four stitches. And here's Allan the evening he left to propose to Cheryl . . . Oh, lookie here! Our first apartment. I can still see that mouse you chased with a broom. That was a riot!"

The good times, the bad times, the happy and sad times, all work together to cement more firmly the relationship of two people who remain committed to each other, more strongly as each year passes.

. . . .

*It is not just luck which holds
a marriage together but hard work.
We both still work at it every day.*

Two families, next-door neighbors, were at the zoo, laughing and apparently enjoying themselves. Later at home, Harry and Maria started to talk. "Do you think the Nestors are always as happy as they looked at the zoo? Sometimes I think Joe looks a bit wistful."

In the Nestor house the mother, Ina, was in the process of getting drunk again, her typical nightly behavior. Joe was making dinner and helping the kids with their schoolwork. Their teenager, Joey, was out for the evening but had not gone where he had told his father he would be. Instead he was in the local park drinking beer and smoking pot with his friends.

Maria gave Harry a hug. "I don't know what goes on over there, honey," he said, "but I bet they aren't as happy as we are. I love you and I always will."

. . . .

What we see is not always the whole truth. I am grateful for the love and caring my family and I share.

Few of us plan to have an affair. Attraction to another person usually is quite accidental. Work or other situations may throw two people together who otherwise would never have been interested in each other.

Once the initial attraction has begun, it takes a very strong person to walk away. Many do. Both men and women walk away from the opportunity and we never even know they turned their backs on temptation.

It is not a natural conclusion that the individual who cast aside this unforseen opportunity has a good or even a strong marriage. It is just that this person is strong enough and feels good enough about his or her character to let good judgment prevail.

. . . .

Choosing what path I will
follow in life is my responsibility.
I can and do make good choices.

Only the young or the very immature expect that all their personal needs for love, affection, physical attention and even financial care can be placed upon one individual. Some of us married with the attitude that we were being "saved" — that we would never need another friend as close as the one we married. Time proved many of us wrong.

Years later, we understood that no one person is responsible for another's well-being. We grew personally and expanded our horizons. Friendships were formed. And we learned to depend upon ourselves. Anything else would have kept us children.

. . . .

*I am an adult and can take care
of my own needs.*

Mistakes. We all make them. Some of us even admit them. One of the hardest mistakes to admit is that we have either married the wrong person or that the person we married did not turn out to be whom we expected.

Some people cannot handle the simple fact of making a mistake. Others use it as a growth process. We need to discover why we made the mistake in the first place. Did we misjudge the person or perhaps our own needs?

It may take professional counseling or maybe a support group, along with a desire not to repeat past performances. But if it matters to us that we learn from our own errors, we can succeed in getting on with our lives.

. . . .

Even though I make some mistakes,
I have the right to learn from them
and get on with my life.

We live hurried and crowded lives these days. Crowded in our homes and apartments. Crowded in the shopping malls. Stressed out on the highways. Rush, rush, all day long.

Tempers can flare when people who care deeply about each other live in such close surroundings — despite their love. Husbands and wives and also our children each need time to be alone. Time to think private thoughts, time to be left alone and, most importantly, time to get to know oneself.

Even in a crowded home, family members can and should learn to respect our individual right to be alone. Take a bath, go for a walk but find a way to give yourself a few moments alone.

. . . .

Today I will give myself the gift
of time to be alone.

When we first realize that we are in a failing relationship, many of us tend to panic. We would just as soon hold on to the known than risk the chance of being out on our own.

For many, the thought of not having a willing arm to lean on makes us feel we stand out like a sore thumb. We can just imagine the comments that might go on behind our backs: "What a pity! They seemed to be so stable. I wonder what happened?"

The fear of what people will say and how we feel when we stand on our own keep many of us in unfulfilling marriages. Only when it gets bad enough, only when we are so unhappy that there seems no viable alternative than to leave, do we begin to accept the inevitability of uncertain feelings.

*I can show my personal strength as
I grow during my separation.*

In our child's mind we carried the image of an ideal marriage. All smiles, no yelling, abundant money and love. Warm nutritious dinners each night, family vacations galore.

Few of us actually experienced such a home life, yet many hope that our love will be the truest, the best and the longest lasting. Our frame of reference is that of a child's and it takes a long while to become adult, to realize how hard it is to develop a relationship.

Time and a great deal of effort are needed to build a new life and as we build we understand what commitment to another person is all about. We must put forth time and effort into making our marriages work.

The dreams of childhood will never be forgotten as I continue to move forward as an adult.

"Do you remember when?" becomes a common thread for a couple who have been together for years. Remember Susie's first communion? And the time our rowboat popped a leak!

A life together is built upon memories. When memories become too sad or bitter and good times are no more, fragile relationships begin to unravel.

Shared memories between family members form the structure of our days and the fabric of our lives. Working together to accept both the good and the bad of life and staying committed to each other are what enable us to remain a family.

. . . .

I am committed to my marriage.
Together we can solve all
of our problems.

We all remember when marriage was for a lifetime but things have changed. Too few couples stay together for life anymore. And worse, too few plan on it. "Oh well, if this doesn't work, I can always get married again!"

The best we can do now is not give up our quest for a strong relationship. Having failed once or even twice does not mean we always will. If marriage matters to us, we must first figure out why we keep failing.

We don't want to repeat our mistakes but we do want to be happy again. Rather than repeat the same mistakes, we can use personal growth to improve those problem areas.

. . . .

From this day forward I will feel
proud that I am letting myself
learn and grow emotionally.

It has been said, "To thine own self be true."
We want to be true to ourselves but sometimes
we don't take the time to listen to our own
needs.

It is quite easy to delude ourselves, to pretend that a problem we know exists just isn't
there at all. We make excuses for the things
which have gone wrong in our lives. "It's not
my fault that I was fired. My boss never appre-
ciated me." Or, "She wouldn't know a good
thing if it kicked her in the face." And, "He
drank too much."

Finally we stop dancing and start listening to
the music. We begin to realize that we are at
fault for much of what happens to us. Changing
our behavior, not scapegoating so much or
blaming our problems on others, gives us a
chance at learning to change.

. . . .

I am responsible for my own life.
As of today, I will be responsible
for all my actions.

How can we help the homeless, we wonder, or women and children who are abused? We are only one; our voice and ability are small. All too often we do nothing and our opportunity to help slides away.

Then the time may come when we are the ones who need help — a grief group, a 12-Step program, for grocery shopping or a willing shoulder to lean on. We understand then, and only then, how each small action, how each willing person, can blend together to help those who need assistance.

By doing what we can, in a very quiet way, we add our strength to that of others and make our first move. We gain immeasurably from the act of giving.

I will not pass up an opportunity to help another human being.

Bearing A Grudge

Injuries heal. Broken bones recover, new skin grows over old. What may not be erased, however, is an act that caused injury. Some people bear grudges, even when an apology has been made. When the injury has gone and the source of anger remains, problems ensue.

We want to feel good about the things we do in our lives. When one person with a grief against us holds onto anger, it causes us to feel uncertain and unhappy.

If the source of anger is from an act we don't understand and can't do anything to change, the relationship will fall apart. It is then that we must let ourselves move on.

. . . .

My own strength surprises me
as I leave my relationship. I know
now I have done nothing wrong.

When we were children, we were very adamant about adult life. "I'm going to make heaps of money," muttered one young woman, while her friend declared, "I'm going to drive fancy cars and own a lot of property."

These are childish notions and it doesn't take long to realize that, at work and in personal relationships, we will do the best we can and no more. Gone are our ideas of wealth, fortune and fame. Instead, taking shape gently as we mature, is the recognition that people are what matter most. People to love and people to care about. Laughter. Joy. Charity. These are the things that really matter. Slowly we reform our old attitudes, realizing that what is most important is the emotional caring that we give to each other unselfishly.

Unselfish giving makes me
feel wonderful.

Now that our marriage or relationship is over
— in many cases shattered — we find ourselves
conducting a silent post-mortem about what
went wrong. This is a very natural thing to do.
For a long while we may berate ourselves for
our role in the breakup.

Sometimes it takes years before we are willing to face the truth. Most of us wanted desperately to please the one we loved. So we com-
promised our desires, our values and often
even our rights as human beings.

When it's over, really over, we begin to saw
through the links that kept us bound together
— chains we never even knew were there. We
take back our individuality, our humanity, our
right to be separate and to feel worthwhile.

. . . .

*I am a valuable and
worthwhile person.*

Some people adapt nervous habits when they are in uncomfortable situations — clenching their teeth, grimacing. The ones who feel the least confident, who have the lowest self-image, may even develop a habit of nervous laughter.

Overt actions often hide deeper, more serious feelings. Each of us, at one time or another, has been embarrassed by the one we love. We have disagreed with words uttered in public but we'd sooner die than criticize back.

Until we are ready to defend ourselves, our deepest feelings and our moral fiber, we will continue to laugh, and laugh and laugh, often with tears in our eyes.

I am finally letting myself deal honestly with my own emotions.

Recently, at the dinner table, conversation turned to childhood. One woman asked if any of her friends had been spanked as kids. Several said yes. Justine said, "My folks never did. They didn't believe in it. Once though, Mom was in a rare bad mood. Maybe she'd had a fight with Dad. I was slapped for spilling milk. She reached across the table and really let me have it. I ran screaming from the room.

"A few minutes later Mom came to my room, crying. 'I'm sorry, honey,' she said as she hugged me. 'I took my problems out on you.' I've never forgotten her quick apology and that she was so ashamed."

Loving someone means admitting you were wrong and saying you are sorry.

. . . .

*I feel proud I can apologize when
I have made an error.*

Even physically abused children will fight when they are taken from their parents. They want to go back, despite the risk of being beaten because the threat of the unknown is worse.

Most of us love our parents unconditionally. At least we did until we became older and began to make judgments about the kind of people our parents really were. It is strange that as we look back upon our childhoods, we first remember the terrible times before we can let ourselves savor the good ones.

As adults we understand that our parents did their best, according to how they were parented. If we wish to break the chain, we must allow ourselves the chance to grow and have the openness to learn new ways.

. . . .

In breaking the chain of abuse, I will make a better world for my children.

In *Fiddler on the Roof,* during one memorable scene as his wife is leaning over a hot stove, Tevye asks, "Do you love me?" "After all these years?" she teases him but finally admits, "Of course I love you."

True love comes from sharing good times and bad. From barely having enough food but eating bread and jelly sandwiches at a happy backyard picnic. From finding joy in situations others would find helpless.

When good times are no more, when only a work ethic prevails, there really is a question of two people tethered just by marriage vows. When playing and laughter are gone, it may be time to give ourselves permission to move on.

Remembering to show how I love
my partner makes me feel
good about myself.

In the olden days women depended on their man completely. This changed when folks traveled west. Women learned to run a homestead and fire a gun, skills they needed to survive.

Most women these days want to be self-sufficient. Out on their own, women are capable of working and supporting themselves. Often this goes one step further, as some women declare they need no one. Changing a tire, doing karate, fixing the plumbing and running the household hardly present a challenge.

Eventually, many women realize that there is more to life than being autonomous. Learning to love does not take away individuality. Life can be greatly enhanced by allowing the risk of loving.

I am no longer afraid to give of myself to another person. Being in love is wonderful.

47

Our needs, desires, goals and lifestyles undergo many changes as we move through the years. Who we were at 18 and who we become at 38 may be totally opposite. When this natural course of events happens, most families can "roll with the punches" and make necessary adjustments.

We hear stories, to the extreme, of mothers and fathers who just get up and leave. They move away, break off entirely from their family and provide no financial or emotional support. Whether living in the north woods alone or becoming a dealer in Las Vegas, there is rarely a reason so strong that one needs to desert one's family.

. . . .

No matter how much I am tempted,
I will never desert my family.

"Stop leaving your nylons on the shower rod," Homer screeched. Essie ran crying from the room, hurt once again by his temper, which flared without any warning. "I don't understand him," she told Sarah. "He drinks, then he yells and gets crude. I can't believe it. I'm sick and tired of this behavior."

What happened between Essie and Homer happens to many of us. Real issues are clouded over by quick bursts of temper. What we need to do is learn to place anger where it belongs. Essie and Homer did love each other. With lots of talking and the help of a marriage therapist, they now stand a strong chance of having a closer, more respectful, loving marriage.

I am learning to share my feelings and place my anger where it belongs.

There was a married couple who danced together so beautifully it looked as if their ankles were tied together. Joy and happiness shone from their faces. They only had eyes for each other.

When two people are committed to a shared life, they understand that devotion and caring aren't automatic. They need to work at it, to keep the gears of their life continuously oiled — to help their marriage run smoothly, to be two halves of a well-oiled machine.

People who truly love and respect each other allow one another the opportunity to function separately. They stand united, never criticizing one another in public, conducting arguments privately. They are a couple, a pair, and they are proud of it.

My spouse and I have a strong marriage because we both love and respect one another.

The midlife crisis. The very words strike terror in our hearts. Perhaps at 40 the inevitability of having to admit who we are and what we have achieved is hard to bear. Rather than make that admission, some choose to create a new and perhaps more interesting lifestyle. Changing professions, finding personal gurus and having extramarital affairs are all common behaviors.

So much can change at midlife. As we reassess our past and look toward our future, some of us might not like what we see. We can use midlife crises to make things right with ourselves. Many years are left. What we do with our time is up to us. Midlife crises can become a very positive time of life.

. . . .

My midlife crisis helped me realize that
I love my family and want to
stay just where I am.

As teenagers we often confused love with lust. Intimate relationships began with fireworks. Later we realize that sex becomes just one aspect of a marriage.

Plunging into a marriage for the physical relationship, for the way the other person looks, for premature pregnancy or for the right to be a twosome should not be the only reasons we marry. A marriage built on such fragile foundations may be doomed to failure.

Physical love just isn't enough. Love that comes with sharing good and bad times, raising children and with being flexible as needs change stands a far better chance for survival. Unconditional love is essential to a successful marriage.

. . . .

Regardless of whether I am happy or angry with my family, I will always love them unconditionally.

Remember the silent movies in which the heroine bats her six-inch eyelashes at having just been rescued off the railroad tracks by a handsome gentleman and proclaims, "My hero!" She is ready to fall into his arms just because he saved her.

There are heroes in every marriage. At one time or another each becomes a hero in the other's eyes. It may be from balancing the budget or from taking an extra job to make ends meet.

The important point is that the balance shifts back and forth constantly. Quietly heroic deeds keep marriages on an even keel. Respect and loving one another are heroic on their own.

. . . .

Our marriage is strong. At times,
each one of us assumes the
position of leadership.

A newly married young woman, at lunch with friends, told them, "I really envy the relationship my in-laws share. They love and cherish each other as much now as they did 40 years ago. I hope we do as well."

We are so often blind when we first marry, blind to each other's faults, blind to our own shortcomings. With the realization that we are not perfect, some of the "rose-colored glasses" effect wears off.

The couple who is truly bound to one another, who believes one marries for life, faces their problems head-on. They talk about what bothers them and they talk about what they like about each other. Talking is the key, for they never give up on their vows. Over and over they talk, sometimes with tears, often with laughter. But they never stop cherishing each other.

. . . .

Even when I am angry or upset, I still love the person I married and I will remember to say so often.

Oh, my! The things we called each other when we were teens! Macho Man. Luscious Lips. Terms we thought were cool. As adults, we know that who we are is not defined by simply how we look. Back then, most of us thought we were so mature.

Years pass by and are filled with many experiences. We wonder how we ever thought we were totally mature since, even now, as adults, we learn more about ourselves each and every day. In life as well as in relationships, we understand now that real maturity is an ongoing process. Move over Macho Man and Luscious Lips! Make room for a grown-up!

I am mature but inside of me is the kid who still believes, just a little, in the mystique of Macho Man and Luscious Lips!

When we were small, many of us sucked our thumbs or had special "blankies" we dragged everywhere we went, much to our parent's consternation. Comfort items were an important part of our lives as children.

Obviously most of us outgrew our need to suck thumbs and drag blankets. What we never outgrew was the need to feel secure and comfortable.

As adults, most of us learn to surround ourselves with comfort items. For one person it might be a new book; for another, a special baseball glove or fishing pole. Going to the movies, complete with candy bars or popcorn helps others feel content. We each find our own comfort.

. . . .

*Feeling comfortable and secure in
my own surroundings is my right, and
one way I help myself handle stress.*

We all make excuses when things go wrong,
sometimes even when we know we have caused
the problem. It is human nature to blame someone else.

Recognizing that we have erred, especially if
we have made a mistake in choosing our life
partner, hurts us too deeply to admit it. We
have a tendency to blame the other person for
what they did, or how they acted. The fact that
we may be enabling or co-dependent or even
just too soft-spoken to get our own needs met
seems irrelevant to us.

When we are willing to admit the fault may
be our own — or at least some of it — when
we begin to find solutions to our failures, we
show our readiness to find new and better ways
to achieve personal success.

. . . .

*Admitting the fault is mine is a giant
step toward personal growth.*

57

The quiet type: a person who doesn't like to share emotions with other people. Pensive and inward, these people are often known as loners.

A warm and long-lasting relationship may enable a loner to open up and begin to trust just enough to talk a bit. For the most part, though, these people keep to themselves and choose jobs which allow them to continue their lonely lifestyle.

Then there is the person who wants to talk, who wants desperately to have close friends and loving relationships but just doesn't know how. This person may be the lucky one, for given time and the willingness to learn — often through professional therapy or support groups — old habits can change and new, more open ones can take their place.

. . . .

It was so important to me to have friends and to feel normal that I risked therapy to come out of my shell.

There is no stuffed animal more famous for giving comfort than a teddy bear. It allows us to abuse it, hug it, cry into its fur and possibly even wear it out. Shown affection as children, we are likely to become affectionate adults. We also learn how much affection to give. Too much, and we are considered emotionally needy. Too little, and we are considered cold.

As adults we recognize there are right and wrong times to show affection. Showing love may have little to do with touching. It has far more to do with acts of kindness and compassion, being there when a friend needs us and treating our fellow human beings as we would wish to be treated.

There is so much more to love than making love. Showing affection is an important facet of my life.

Mothers have passed it on for millenium: "Don't do it if it feels wrong." Many unkind acts have been aborted as we remembered the admonishment.

However, when it comes to love, all that we have learned at our mother's knee flies right out of the window. There is an indefinable something that occurs between two people who are falling in love. We know now that the physical attraction is more subtle than we thought and can be based, among other things, upon the smell of the other person.

We follow our hearts, we follow the "bells ringing" and respond to the flowers. The pain of love can be exquisite, running every gamut of emotion from joy to despair.

....

*The joy and glory of being in love
cause my heart to soar.*

Twice divorced, he leaned upon his elbow and lamented, "I just can't believe my marriage is over. What do I keep doing wrong?" What, indeed, we wonder, as we muse over our own failures at close loving relationships.

Some people repeat the pattern again and again. We hear of third and fourth and fifth marriages. For some, the success is in being married, not in becoming the best person we can become.

It is not easy to change old habits but that's just what we must do when we repeat problem behavior. Deciding something is wrong with the way we relate and then making a plan to change is often a long and painful process. But eventually we will create change and our relationships will take on new meaning.

. . . .

Marriage is important to me and
I will do what is necessary
to change old habits.

Sometimes we just get worn out. Belligerent teenagers, not having enough money to pay bills, dealing with mental illness and fighting with in-laws are some of the reasons we grow emotionally weary. Some buckle under the stress and shut down emotionally. They get up, go to work and come home — never reaching out to family, hiding behind a newspaper or upstairs in the bedroom.

People who stay and fight for their rights, who never give up, who learn about Tough Love and who get part-time jobs to help with the finances, seem to be the ones who hang on to their own sanity. It's not easy to be part of the fracas but at least they don't withdraw. These folks have learned to live their own lives as well as they can without giving away their own sanity.

. . . .

As a family, we all need to pull together
in crises, large and small.

While strolling through a local park on a warm spring day, one can observe dozens of young people. They are walking together, arms intertwined, bodies joined, it seems, at the hip. Faces gleaming, eyes locked upon each other, euphoria emanating from every vein: love like this warms us.

These young people believe that they have found the person who is best suited to be their mate. We might have many of these young loves as we grow up.

As adults we learn that physical love is but a small part of a relationship. Compatability, both intellectual and social, as well as common interests and moral values, is what really bind two people together. Still let us never forget how wonderful young love can feel.

. . . .

*I cherish the value and memory of
each relationship I have had.*

There are always two sides of the coin. Some people can slough off troubles while others take problems a bit more seriously. Going to extremes is certainly not the answer, yet many of us do. We become so intense that we create problems in our relationships by not being willing to let go, even for a little while. Sometimes it can become a power struggle.

As with everything else, we need to strike a balance. Of course we will worry. One can hardly escape from it. By learning to modulate our feelings, to set aside time for worry and to discuss troublesome topics, we can find time for other dimensions of our life as well.

I know I worry too much. I am struggling to give perspective to my problems.

It is amazing that we have attached feelings of love to the human heart — which is really just a muscle to pump blood. We use phrases such as, "Have a little heart" or "You gotta have heart," or "That person is heartless."

Through modern technology, one person's heart can be placed into another person's chest cavity and will function just as well in its new home.

Even with a new heart, what really separates us as human beings is our wonderful, unique individuality. All the facets that combine to make us who we are, kind or mean, giving or cruel, empathetic or harsh, are what make each and every one of us different from the other.

Each person is so different. I know there is someone out there who is the perfect mate for me.

We see them on the television and cringe. Feeling thankful that it's not our family who is involved, we reluctantly watch people cry at their children's funerals or see them being interviewed after horrible plane crashes. Life is full of tragedy. But bearable when it isn't ours.

People whom we thought were friends seem, in our eyes, delighted to spread the bad word about our separation. This hurts us, since no matter what the state of our marriage, it's awful when the final breakup comes. Human tragedy, *our tragedy,* is so very hard to handle.

. . . .

Eventually I will recover from
my tragedy and find my
strength again.

Swinging on the tire hanging in the backyard, going up and down on the seesaw, running up the stairs and down the slide, these are some of the wonderful memories of childhood.

As adults we might bowl or walk around the lake. Handicrafts or concerts could be more our cup of tea. Still we play and still we savor life. It's just that as adults we have also learned to balance play and work.

Too many times, as we become embroiled in paying bills, raising children, doing volunteer work, cleaning and repairing the house, we forget how to play. When life gets too serious, we get into trouble. Relationships stay strong when there is a balance, when each makes time for the many facets of their partner's life. Play (as well as music) is the food of love.

Playing keeps me balanced and sane. I will always try to remember to play.

So many of us read love poems when we were in high school. Remember wondering what it would be like to be loved so dearly? The blinders that we wear when we first fall in love slowly disappear as we deal with everyday problems. Difficult in-laws, a father who is an alcoholic, teenagers who alternately drive us nuts and make us proud, these are all common situations that remove the initial blinders of love.

The trick is to keep on going by never forgetting how much we love each other, and always find time to express that love. It doesn't have to be a rose on a pillow; instead it may be waffles on Sunday, doing the wash, or giving a compliment or even a hug.

Counting the ways I can show love to my spouse will never end.

"I'll never forgive him for what he did to me," is an all-too-common cry. Sexual abuse or any kind of abuse, for that matter, is one reason why children grow up hating their parents.

We really have two choices. If we never forgive them, the anger we carry will fester and we will likely become bitter adults, and take out that anger on the people we care about.

The other choice is to see a therapist. This is not easy but the end result can be worth all the tears and all the expense. Now, as grown-ups, we can decide to forgive and let go. We may never have a relationship with that parent but at least we have peace of mind and know that we are finally taking care of ourselves.

. . . .

It took me years to forgive. Now
that I have, new doors
are open to me.

Ideally, we anticipate that marriage will last forever. In love we expect each to contribute fairly to marriage. Ups and downs are an expected part of life but when the down part stays down and our loved one stops contributing to the family, trouble is bound to develop. Even if communication and affection end, some would remain committed if they thought things would improve.

Apart from illness, when one partner stops sharing, when the ties that bind become the ties that restrict, when the situation feels hopeless, there is a huge decision to make: to stay and be unhappy or to take the risk and leave. It is a highly personal decision, one that can only be made with a great deal of agony.

I feel strong and proud that I had the courage to leave a failing marriage.

Our religious, social and cultural values are totally unique to each individual. How our parents raised us, what their backgrounds were and where they came from all influenced the kind of person we became.

Some parents share the discipline. In some families the mother rules the roost, while in others, the father has the final say.

A serious problem may develop when a woman who was raised one way marries a man whose family was just the opposite. Unless the young couple is ready and willing to create new patterns, sparks are going to fly. In creating a union, we create a new set of rules which works out for the better when we learn to compromise.

. . . .

We care so much about each other that it has been easy to compromise.

71

"But Dad, I'm in love with her." A long and serious talk ensues about marrying "beneath" oneself. "No one ever finished high school in that family and your friend won't either."

The child often has his way, for we parents do love our children and want them to be happy. The first months or years may be wedded bliss. Then the trouble begins. One adult becomes more skilled and better educated. The other may have few interests and less skills.

Marrying "beneath" oneself is not really the issue. Marrying a person without goals, who has no desire for personal growth or fulfillment is the problem. There must be a sense of sharing one's future for a marriage to continue to thrive.

. . . .

Leaving my marriage gave me options for a better future. Sometimes parents do know best.

During new love, the couple can feel so exclusive about each other that they will not go out with other friends. Girl friends forsake each other, males ignore the "guys" they've always hung around with.

After the first year or two of marriage, we begin to make friends apart from our "couple" friends. When the husband or wife will not accept the other's friends, problems arise.

When individual friendships are not tolerated, both husband and wife need to talk over their options. Must the friend be given up altogether or can there be a compromise? Is it possible to go out alone with that friend to a game or shopping? Our close friendships are important for emotional survival.

. . . .

I have a right to have friends
but must be careful not to
exclude my loved one.

Married for a few years, the time seemed right to have a baby. You can imagine Judy's surprise when Ralph said, "I've been thinking. I don't want children." Taken aback, Judy ran crying from the room. Later, when she calmed down, they made coffee and talked. "When we were dating, you never registered any objection to kids. Why now?" Ralph explained that he was abused as a child by both his parents. "Since I have a short fuse, too, I'm afraid I'll do the same thing."

Over the months Ralph would neither budge, compromise nor go for counseling. Judy was distraught. Gathering all her emotional strength, Judy left her marriage. She loved Ralph but couldn't imagine an entire life without children.

*Leaving my marriage was an
agonizing decision but I had
to do what felt right to me.*

It appeared that Cassie and Bob had an ideal relationship. They shared the same religion, had nearly identical interests, had both graduated from college, worked in similar fields and spent long periods of time laughing and talking together.

Slowly, during the months and years after their marriage, Bob's behavior began to erode Cassie's confidence. He shamed her in public for no apparent reason and often told her women were worthless. Cassie realized that he was abusing her, but she also knew she was letting him.

Setting out to improve her damaged self-confidence, she joined a 12-Step program, along with an assertiveness-training class. These classes gave her faith in herself and she no longer allowed herself to be abused.

. . . .

I have learned that I am both strong and important. I will never be pushed around again.

Jennifer loved her husband, yet she found herself having an affair. Sneaking around to meet another man gave her a thrill. In her waitress job, she told herself, the men seemed to fall all over her. One day a neighbor saw her with a strange man and told Perry. He was hurt and angry and especially worried about her promiscuity. He could neither forgive nor forget. For months he stayed because of the children. Then he divorced her, got custody and moved away.

Perry loved his wife dearly and felt they had a wonderful marriage. It wasn't until he got some professional help that he realized it wasn't his fault at all and that he, in no way, had caused her behavior.

. . . .

Even though I loved my wife, I needed
to leave for myself, for my children
and for my sanity.

Sarah wandered through the house she and her beloved Ross had planned and built together. Touching the vase he'd bought her while they were in Hawaii, she couldn't help but wonder why they had fallen out of love.

Running her hand over the small, owl-shaped piece of driftwood they had found in northern Minnesota, she began to cry. "Neither of us did anything wrong. We didn't have affairs and we hardly ever spent any time apart. Why did this have to happen?"

Time does begin to heal all wounds and months later they both realized they had been far too complacent in assuming their marriage was forever.

. . . .

If I ever remarry, I will never again
take anyone for granted.

Peering into shop windows and having a leisurely stroll down the main street of her small town, Hillary passed a small Italian restaurant. On impulse, she decided to have an early lunch of veal parmesan. Contented and full she climbed into her car and burst into tears. She suddenly realized it was that same Italian restaurant where Roger, her ex-husband, proposed. "Why would I care?" she thought. "I'm better off without him."

Even if we don't want to admit it, we all hold memories that are special to us. They were important parts of our lives and being divorced just doesn't make the good times go away.

I have a right to remember good times and to feel badly because my relationship ended.

After we marry and especially after we have children, we understand the importance of life insurance and making out wills. We don't want to risk our children's care or their inheritance.

The hurt of being divorced, whether the marriage was a strong one or whether it started on shaky legs, stays with us for years. Most of us try hard to move on to new relationships. We would really like to put the past aside.

It is at this vulnerable time that we must change our wills and insurance beneficiaries. We would rather not think about these matters but it would be tragic to have the man or woman to whom we were once married inherit whatever estate we leave behind.

. . . .

*Even though I hate to think about wills
and insurance beneficiaries, I will still
take care of these matters quickly
so I need not worry.*

If we have had a hard time going through our separation and divorce, and if a feeling of relief washes over us now that it is over, most likely we will revel in the glory of being alone.

At first, when we are alone again, it is a delicious feeling. Before too long, boredom will set in. Then it is time to get back into society. Tentative at first, out of practice on how to meet people, we find it takes a while to find our niche — to feel comfortable with our new role.

There are lots of people who would like to have a new friend. Once we begin making new friends, both male and female, we wonder what it was we were worrying about.

. . . .

Now that I have begun making new friends there is no stopping me!

Both people involved suffer in a divorce. They suffer from loss of companionship, especially if children were involved. They suffer financially, but most importantly, they miss the person who used to be their best friend.

If the man or woman has to pay alimony for any length of time, this person's level of income goes down considerably. If the ex-husband or wife has a chronic illness, that presents a new and very complicated set of financial and emotional issues.

In today's society, it is often the woman who is less educated and who becomes the newly impoverished. With little money and less ability, she suffers tremendously from her divorce.

. . . .

It is not easy to be divorced.
I remind myself daily that I was
not happily married.

When parents do not share information that their children have already become aware of, such as money trouble, poor health or marital problems, they do a great disservice to their kids.

By not sharing this information, rather than protecting youngsters from hurt, the parents are depriving the children of the truth — as well as the right to learn how to handle problems which arise within the family. Children need security, which is often gained from knowing the truth.

If the parents weren't so secretive about family matters, the children could learn how to successfully deal with internal family problems.

. . . .

Children are entitled to know
about family matters and need
to be part of the solutions.

Sitting in the psychiatrist's office, Harrison found himself in tears. He had been talking about his former wife. "I just don't understand. If we weren't good for each other anymore, why do I feel so melancholy? When I think about what we had and how it was, I really get sad."

The doctor explained that what Harrison was feeling was normal. After all, he had been in love with his wife for many years and they had shared many wonderful memories together. Being divorced doesn't take away shared memories. Letting yourself remember the better times, the fun times, is a good way to validate your own decision.

*Sometimes I have to feel sad
to feel better.*

Forced Civility

After the divorce was made final, after the papers were signed, the newly divorced may have a hard time being civil to each other. When they do talk, harsh words may spring unbidden from their lips. Family members, especially the children, don't want to be around people who fight all the time.

Often because of the children or because of financial issues or paperwork that needs to be completed, the newly divorced have to see each other once in a while.

Remembering that we made the decision, as adults, to end our marriage reminds us that we really do know how to behave properly. For the sake of those who love us, we all need to call a truce while around others.

. . . .

My failure at marriage should not be carried into public places.

Walking through their old house, Dean and Gerri began to reminisce. They remembered, together, the good times they shared while fixing up the house. Sanding the stairs and sneezing constantly. The time the cat died under the front porch.

Their children, who had come to help pack, were surprised to see their newly divorced parents smiling at old shared memories. "I hope this is how you two will get along now that you are divorced," stated their college-age son. "I hear some people can be better friends divorced than they were married."

It is quite amazing that once conflict is removed, once they no longer live together, some couples become friends again.

. . . .

While we just could not live together,
we can still care deeply
for one another.

Most people consider themselves fairly good parents. They cooperate in parenting and try to stand united in the way they discipline. When their relationship is terminated, they talk it over and still intend to share parenting.

What happens, then, when two people who had agreed on childcare issues change their ways once a divorce occurs? In extreme cases, one parent may feel entitled to do all the parenting and could possibly try to kidnap the children. One parent constantly undermines the other's efforts and the children become the ones who suffer. Promises are forgotten and everyone is unhappy.

. . . .

*I intend to be honorable when keeping
my promises to my children
and to my ex-partner.*

The first thing people want to know when a relationship ends is why? Some speculate: "They probably fought all the time." Or, "I hear she was heavily into drugs." Gossipers love fuel for their fodder and bad news always travels fast.

We never cease to be surprised when people who have been casual friends all of a sudden call us every day. These folks are "crisis lovers." They want to be in the thick of things and are gone again when the crisis is over. Why do some people beg for the lurid details of a marriage gone bad?

It is not easy when we finally make the decision to separate or divorce. No matter how difficult it had become, there is a secret part of us that still wishes it had worked. We were in love once and this is such a final and irrevocable move.

. . . .

It is best for me not to share any intimate details except with those people I have known and trusted for years.

Every human being has basic needs that must be met. These are food, clothing, shelter and touch. The first three are generally provided without question. Touch is too often ignored. By many, touch is considered to be crucial to survival.

Babies need to get the message that they are wanted and will be cared for. One way in which parents can do this is to gently stroke the baby, caress its tiny fingers and toes, snuggle into its wonderfully soft cheeks.

Adults need affection, too. One of the complaints of widows, widowers and divorced people is that no one hugs them. No matter what the problems were in our marriage, most of us occasionally got some physical affection. That's one reason we held on for so long.

. . . .

Now that I am alone, I need to find
my hugs from friends and relatives,
and from doing volunteer work
that makes me feel good.

As children, we were accustomed to the way our own family functioned. Since we never lived with anyone but our own parents, we had no basis for comparison until we were old enough to observe other families.

In many of our homes we received mixed messages from our parents. Some problem or another, perhaps some form of addiction or a promiscuous parent, got glossed over throughout our childhood.

When we pretend nothing is wrong and continue to smile and act as though everything is perfect, we deprive ourselves of the honesty that creates balance in our lives.

. . . .

My marriage would have been a great deal easier if we had been able to talk about our difficulties.

Time hangs heavy on our hands. Now that we are truly alone we're not sure that we want to be. For a while, some of us get frantic in our need to stay away from home. Shopping, traveling, jogging, sports and other pursuits keep us busy.

Eventually, we will have to face the empty house. We find that we miss the companionship of another person at home. Forming new routines not based on anyone else's schedule is a difficult adjustment to make.

It's hard to create a completely new lifestyle, one that includes new friends and new activities. Making home a pleasant place helps as well as rearranging furniture, painting, gardening and placing pictures where you want them to be. Eventually, we learn to be comfortable with our own company.

. . . .

It is quite difficult to spend so much
time with myself but I am
struggling to learn.

April Fool's Day. As children, we pulled all the tricks — such as salt in the sugar bowl and "Look, there's a spider in your milk!" As adults we know that April is a wonderful month to help us notice that spring is rapidly approaching. With spring comes renewal.

Spring is a wonderful time of the year to get in touch with both nature and with our own spiritual feelings. All too often, especially if we have been feeling unhappy, we have a tendency to let our relationship with both nature and with our Higher Power slip away.

April 1st is a fine day to affirm choices we have made in the past and to look forward to renewed spirituality and the fresh blossoms of spring.

. . . .

The renewal of the grass and flowers
is a fine time to renew my
belief in a Higher Power.

It's a problem we all face. Now divorced and single, we hardly remember what it was like to date. What are the rules now? Some make the decision to do nothing until they are ready. Others say they'll never get married again and won't even venture into the dating community.

Whatever we choose, most of us eventually want to date, to have a worthwhile relationship with a member of the opposite sex. There are all sorts of community organizations to help us; Parents Without Partners is one good example. Many community centers, churches and social groups have programs for the newly divorced.

. . . .

*Reaching out was not easy, but when I
finally did it, I found that there were
other people who have been
just as lonely as I.*

Small issues. One is a vegetarian and the other will eat only red meat and potatoes. The husband loves board games and cards; she considers them a waste of time. Small things but a real bother in their marriage. Their common grounds are slowly being chipped away.

One evening, Red and Trudy had a long talk. "Honey, we don't have much in common anymore. All we do together is sleep in the same bed."

"What are you saying, Trudy? Do you want to separate?"

They both thought about it for weeks and mutually agreed that they really didn't share their lives anymore. They decided on a trial separation. They were two adults parting as friends. It was a very hard decision but one they both felt better about making.

. . . .

Parting as friends left us both feeling
good about our decision.

Chatty Cathy, they called her. She was a non-stop talker. In fact, her chatter was what attracted Stuart to her in the first place. With six kids, Kathy was primarily a homemaker. Theirs was a busy and happy home, filled with kids, cookies and laughter. One by one the children grew up and moved away.

The house was quiet now — and Cathy chattered on. One day Stuart yelled, "Will you shut up! For 20 years I've hated how you rattle on. I can't stand it."

Cathy was stunned and hurt. She whispered, tears running down her face, "If I've been bothering you all this time, why didn't you tell me before? You shouldn't have waited until you had to explode."

. . . .

We would do much better if we could
talk about our problems before
they reach a crisis state.

Sabotage

While we are often trim as youths, if we don't make exercise a lifestyle, extra pounds creep up. Men lose easily. Women can diet again and again, only to gain back lost pounds.

Sulynn lost weight easily but always gained it back. Finally, frustrated and angry, she was committed to keeping it off. Analyzing why she had trouble, she came to the conclusion that each time she lost weight, Ray would sabotage her efforts: "Let's go out for pizza." Or, "I brought you home a candy bar." Obviously Ray didn't want his wife to be thin.

Often deep-seated reasons can destroy well-conceived plans. Constant sabotage may lead to ruined marriages as the sabotaged spouse eventually figures it out.

. . . .

*I will lose weight for myself and I will
keep it off for the same reason.*

"Do you promise to love, honor and cherish this person, for better or for worse, in sickness and in health, until death do you part?"

After the first glorious year, we begin to settle down. Still loving, still committed, but less physical and more into the relationship, communication and building a life together.

At this time we begin to discover faults and annoying habits we never noticed before. Strongly committed people solve their differences and move on with their marriage.

What happens when we realize that our marriage is failing? We expected it to be like Ward and June Cleaver's, happy and loving. In reality, it isn't that way. Broken promises and broken dreams are too much for some people to bear and they sadly go their separate ways.

. . . .

The promises and dreams we planned still
taunt me when I realize that our
marriage is truly broken
beyond repair.

"Mom, tell me about how you and Daddy met." Her brother coaxed his mom as well. "Yeah, tell us, please?" "No! I don't want to talk about your father. He's a no-good bum. Don't ever ask me to talk about him again!"

It may hurt to talk, but we were once both madly in love, and by refusing to tell the children about the wedding and the early years, we deprive them of their own history.

It's okay to say, "We had an unhappy marriage because your father abused me. I made him leave when you were small." Kids have a right to know and, especially, to hear good memories. We need to answer without being nasty.

. . . .

I can be truthful without
being vengeful.

It was an amiable separation. Shirley and Brock sat down and talked it all over like two adults. The marriage was over. Now it was a matter of tying up loose ends. "Okay with joint custody? We'll each have the kids two weeks."

"Sounds okay with me. What about the furniture? You take the dining room set. I'd like the rocking chair and the bedroom set."

"Oh, I want to keep the dog."

"Rover? Over my dead body! I'll sue you. How could you? I want that dog and I'll do whatever it takes to get him."

There is just no accounting for human emotions. This couple had reached an impasse and their amiable divorce turned out not to be so pleasant after all.

. . . .

Giving up my dog is the last straw.
I just can't back down.

Commonly, we forget any of the good times we shared when we have just divorced. In fact, the angered and bereaved party is often so incensed at the hurt and pain caused by a sudden divorce that angry words spew forth like molten lava. This happens often. The problem begins when the lava spreads over anyone who gets in its path.

Naturally, we are hurt and angry. Seeing a therapist to deal with our feelings will help, so will keeping a journal. One man wrote a hate letter every night to his former wife, scribbling all the nasty thoughts he had and then, afterward, stood over the sink and burned it. It's hard not to be upset after a divorce.

. . . .

I need to remember I am an adult.
It is not appropriate to dump my hurt
feelings onto someone else.

All of a sudden two adults find themselves sparring in front of the children about adolescent issues. The father might say, "I just can't give you child support this month. I don't have any extra money." Maturity goes out the window as one parent takes the children to the zoo in the rain or buys forbidden treats.

Letting a young child stay up late so one is not the villainous parent may work for a short while but in the long run it is damaging. Children need and want discipline. Knowing that they have two mature parents who stand together on raising the kids, even after the divorce, will help smooth the way for a better adjustment and happier children.

. . . .

My children have already been hurt
immeasurably by the divorce.
I do not want to hurt them further
with my immaturity.

"I should have known," Betty told Donna. "He started coming home late from work. I believed that he was working late on a project."

There are clues when a person is having an affair, signs we just don't recognize until they nearly slap us in the face.

Getting a new hair style is one, as is buying new clothes or paying more attention to appearance. One man told me he figured out his wife was involved with a lover when she bought all new nightgowns and underwear.

Some people feel that when their spouse has an affair, their marriage is automatically over. Others look the other way. There are no hard and fast rules. Some can forgive and forget, others cannot.

. . . .

I felt I could never trust my husband again.
It took tremendous strength
on my part to leave.

Getting divorced is like jumping into a tub filled with ice. No matter how we prepared, no one warned us of the unbelievable aftershock. Even saying, "Good. We're better off separated" doesn't take away the inevitable sense of loss we feel.

We all still secretly carry the love we had for each other years before. Since occasionally we dream about our ex, we must need to release hidden feelings. Intellectually it is one thing to say, "I know it's over" and "It's for the better." Emotionally believing it is another thing. It takes a long time but the dreams get fewer and farther between. We do move on to a new lifestyle. There is life after divorce!

. . . .

For months I felt numb
but I am coming alive again and
am ready to move on.

Garlic shrimp and pasta primavera. Until Molly saw the recipe, she thought she was doing fine. As she turned the page, she remembered how Wally loved to entertain friends at dinner, planning, shopping and preparing the meals together.

Molly made herself a cup of tea, sat down to read and burst into tears. Every day she felt more sad. "You're getting depressed. It happens to lots of people after a big change like divorce," her sister had said. Molly wondered if her big sister could be right.

Molly saw a therapist. The doctor listened and agreed she sounded depressed and prescribed an anti-depressant. We can become depressed when we have undergone a major life-change. We owe it to ourselves to seek professional help.

. . . .

Feeling depressed is nothing to be ashamed of. When I asked for help, I knew things would be all right.

It seemed as if everyone was doing it. Placing ads in the personals seemed to be the "in" thing these days. "DWM wants new female friend to walk around the lake with, to attend concerts and sporting events. Light drinker, no smoking. Disease-free. Call: 123-4567."

Bobbi placed an ad and got lots of calls. Nervously she agreed to meet a man in a local bar. This was her first date in 12 years. He seemed nice, so they went to her apartment to have another drink. He pushed her around. Terrified, she screamed and fought but he raped her.

Bobbi did not follow common sense. He knew her address so she changed her locks, not to speak of the terror she was forced to live with.

. . . .

In my eagerness to date again,
I must not cast aside good
common sense.

It is quite normal, occasionally, to bend our interests so that our spouse can have his or her own way. A movie we don't want to see but do anyway, going out for Chinese food, joining in yard work or lovemaking — it doesn't matter. We say okay just to keep the peace.

When one partner has all the say and the other has none, it is often indicative of poor self-esteem and a lack of assertiveness for the submissive person.

Learning to say no or "I really would prefer not to" is not an easy process. Community education classes offer assertiveness training which is good for both men and women. Old habits die hard but we can change that and learn to stand up for ourselves.

. . . .

For too long I have been a doormat.
I am going to learn to stand
up for myself.

Finding out suddenly that an old friend is newly divorced is a difficult situation. People know how traumatic it is but aren't sure what to say.

Consequently, we find ourselves, newly divorced, being hurt by the very person who is attempting to give us sympathy and understanding. All too often we hear phrases like, "You're better off without him" and "I could never understand why you chose to marry such a weird person." People aren't trying to be mean. They just don't know what to say. They want us to know they care but go about it the wrong way.

We can stop their behavior if it makes us uncomfortable, by telling them so. Also, we can help by offering a more gentle, creative way to respond. "I still miss him but it will be better for both of us this way."

By sharing what I feel, I can help pave the way for others who will travel this difficult road.

We knew it was over long before it ended. We didn't want to admit that we had made the wrong choice, that we couldn't live with the person we once loved. We procrastinated for a long time before our final decision was made.

In a sense we feel relieved. Living alone but happy is easier than living in conflict. Conflict tends to create high levels of stress which isn't good for our health.

So why do so many of us launch into the "if only" syndrome? "If only I had talked to her earlier about how I was feeling." "If only we had discussed our sexual problems." If only . . . if only . . . if only. To some extent, we all do it. We have to hash it out in our own minds to convince ourselves that we made an okay decision.

. . . .

Sad though I am that our marriage is over, I feel a sense of relief and peace. I will be all right.

Rita had just divorced — for the third time. She was angry with her failure. "What am I doing wrong? What makes my marriages fail?"

After thinking for days, Rita made an appointment with a counselor. She was scared, not only about the expense but because she didn't know what she would find out. Like many of us, Rita slowly discovered that most of her problems stemmed from childhood. The youngest child of an alcoholic father, she had subordinated her own needs to take care of him.

Her therapist guided her to an ACoA group. Between the group and the therapist, Rita began to understand her behavior. If she chose to marry again, she would, for the first time, stand a chance of success.

. . . .

I am discovering why my marriages
have failed and I do not want
to repeat my mistakes.

Let's face it, most of us like being part of a partnership, half of a couple. This is a world made for "two's." In restaurants the host or hostess isn't always happy seating "singles." Those of us who go alone are aware that it seems as if everyone has someone, except us. People in love seem to be everywhere.

This is a major adjustment once we have separated or have gone through a divorce. Some people solve their problems by staying home for long periods of time, only venturing out for work and grocery shopping. Others keep busy so they are rarely home.

Single is what we are right now, for a short while, or perhaps forever. Each one of us has self-worth; we are important.

I am not afraid to live my life and go on about my business. I care about myself.

109

Each one of us brings to our marriage all that we learned in our parents' home. Since all of our parents had fights at one time or another, we tend to carry those patterns along to our new marriage.

The problem arises when we each fight differently. Perhaps the husband is a sulker, going off to the privacy of the bedroom; while she may be a screamer, following him, yelling, right into their bedroom.

Unless they learn to fight constructively and fairly, they will continue this pattern their whole marriage. Fighting fair is learning to talk about the problems before they escalate, giving each other a chance to explain why they are angry and then figuring solutions out together. And besides, making up is half the fun!

Fighting fairly gives us each a chance
to share our feelings. I will try to
be fair as often as possible.

He didn't really want to go on the date. Bucky just wasn't ready yet but his friends practically forced the issue. Bucky couldn't remember a time in his life, except at 16, when he felt so uncomfortable about going out with a woman.

He was relieved when he saw her because she was cute, but when she opened her mouth it was all over. Her voice had a high-pitched squeal and she reeked of cigarette smoke. Oh, boy, what a long evening.

Bucky knew it was too soon to start dating. But, more importantly, he realized that when he was ready to go out again, he would choose the woman he wanted to go out with. "Blind dates are not for me."

*I will decide when I am ready to
date again and I will decide
whom I will date.*

For the recently divorced, there are often financial issues that have to be considered. When a two-income family becomes single-income, especially if there are children, financial adjustments can always be a problem.

At first, this can be a source of resentment. It takes careful budgeting and cutting back to make ends meet. April solved her problem creatively. She decided to set up a neighborhood barter system. She got Sheldon to mow her lawn and trim her shrubs; she did his washing and ironing. She baked bread for Sally who was glad to do April's mending.

With baby-sitting exchanges, potluck dinners and other barters, April and several other singles all gained. Not only did they help each other financially but they all enjoyed the unexpected bonus of becoming friends.

. . . .

Creative solutions like bartering
help me get through the hard
times after my divorce.

It never occurred to us that our wedding vows might be taxed more than we could ever imagine. Such is the case when one partner becomes chronically ill.

Peter developed Parkinson's disease and as it progressed, he had to leave his job. Before long, Sally was caring for him — just a little at first, then more as the years passed. It wasn't easy but she was committed totally to Peter.

One day, Winston asked how they managed. "It's hard work, Win, but what keeps us going is that we love each other and we both have a good sense of humor. Peter and I laugh often and loudly and we still share many good times. His illness, although inconvenient, is only one facet of our lives together."

Loving each other and laughing together help us keep our sanity in this uncomfortable situation.

One unfortunate side effect of a relationship's breaking apart is that relatives are forced to take sides. In some cases, it doesn't matter, since we are happy not to have those people to deal with.

The problem arises when we really love and miss the person who has pulled away. Whether it is the brother-in-law or mother-in-law, when the separation causes us to lose a good friend, we feel sad and helpless.

In some cases, the relationship ends just because people don't know the new rules. We might be able to rescue our friendship if we were to sit down and have a heart-to-heart conversation. "I know this is awkward but as long as my marriage problems stay taboo as a topic of conversation, there is no reason why we can't stay friends."

. . . .

Divorce is hard enough without
losing close friends. I will work hard
to hang on to my friendships.

Once in a while a husband and wife work together in the family business. Not only are they together at home, but also for eight additional hours at work. In the best of circumstances, this may present problems. In the worst case, it can be devastating to a relationship.

Unless they are the most unusual of married couples, the only solution to spending each day, all day, together, is to develop a set of unwritten rules, often over a period of time, about how each will act toward the other. Marital spats should be saved for the privacy of home since no one is comfortable being caught in the middle of a fight.

At home, when the office doors have been locked, all bets are off and the two who work together, hopefully in peace, can behave however they like in private.

*I enjoy working with my spouse
and I will continue to act
professionally at work.*

Extra Marital Stress

One of the worst strains ever to be placed on a marriage is when a child is born severely handicapped. All the excitement and anticipation of having a healthy child disappear as the couple adjusts to and learns to love their special child.

It has been proven that, time and time again, the strain of a handicapped child is more than most marriages can bear. Divorce rates are astronomical.

There are couples who do make it, who are strengthened by their need to work together. These are the special ones, often the religious ones, who would make it through any crisis and still come out loving each other in the end.

. . . .

Our handicapped child has brought us closer together than ever.

It was as plain as the nose on your face: Patricia and Arthur were growing apart. It wasn't anything overt but their interests were changing and they did less and less together.

One afternoon over coffee, they discussed a trial separation. Both were taken aback at what they were actually considering and both agreed the answer was no. Now Pat and Art had to figure out what to do.

They spent hours finding their common ground, developing new hobbies they both could share. Remembering their courtship days, they planned to recapture some of the fun they had shared, with sports, theater and jigsaw puzzles. Before long, they were inseparable again.

. . . .

We love each other and worked hard to recapture some of the missing joy in our marriage. We are a success story.

It wasn't an easy situation. Earl's job offer, in high-tech computers, was back East. Marilyn's offer was to be vice-president of a bank in Texas.

After agonizing for weeks, they both decided to keep their jobs for a trial period of one year and to be a modern–day commuting couple. Since there were no children, it was easier to make that decision but it was hard on their marriage.

Both Marilyn and Earl had to learn to be especially attentive of each other's needs, even on the phone. They took care to praise each other and to be good listeners. On weekends, when they could be together, neither brought home any work. It wasn't easy but they were doing okay.

....

*If we can live through a year of being
a commuting family, we can live through
anything. Love and careful planning
conquer most problems.*

Once the baby is born and maternity leave has elapsed, most women these days want to go back to work. In some instances, the father decides to stay home and take care of the baby.

This is generally quite a workable situation, provided the father does not become resentful of staying home. It can be hard on a man who used to have a good job when his wife now "brings home the bacon" and he no longer has an income.

It all depends upon how the couple handles it. If the paycheck is referred to as "theirs," if they share the load when she comes home and if he feels proud of his accomplishments as a homemaker, then everyone concerned is happy.

. . . .

Together we are doing a fine job
of providing for the baby
and for each other.

"There are enough problems in this world than for the two of you to get married. Different religions will cause you nothing but grief," shouted Ellie's father as he slammed his fist down on the kitchen table.

Jewish and Catholic — quite a combination but Ellie and Geoff knew they could pull it off. They loved each other and both believed in God. If they had to pray in separate houses of worship, then so be it.

When children came along, they formed their own new family traditions. The children were taught about, and allowed to celebrate, both Christmas and Hanukkah. They went to church with their dad and to synagogue with their mom. This worked out well for all of them.

Mixing religions is difficult but with love and sharing, we have made it work.

For fifty years the grandma and grandpa had been married. They had a beautiful party for their family and friends, and renewed their marriage vows. Everyone had a wonderful time, especially the honorees.

It was plain to see that they adored each other after all these years. Kevin, their great-grandson, asked his grandparents for advice on staying happy, since his own wedding was only a few months away.

"That's easy, son. Never go to bed mad. Remember to touch and hug each other often and talk about your problems before you have to fight about them. And say 'I love you' several times each day."

I will follow my grandparents' advice.
I will work hard to have a marriage
as strong as theirs.

George had just walked into the house when Charlene handed him the new baby. "Do you have any idea how hard it is to take care of this screaming child all day? I can't handle this anymore." With that she began to sob.

It didn't take a genius to figure out something was seriously wrong. George arranged a sitter for the next day, took time off and went with Charlene to her doctor. "Post-partum depression, quite common. We'll give her some medication to help."

Time, patience, love and medicine caused the depression to lift. These were not easy weeks but George understood Charlene had a physical problem that would take time to heal. Offering assistance whenever he could, he saw family life gradually getting better.

. . . .

I was scared for my wife and for the baby
when she got depressed. Being there to
help made me feel better.

That's it — they decided once and for all to end their marriage. They just couldn't be together for five minutes without fighting with each other.

Husband and wife no more, they both moved on to find a new way of life. The problem, however, was that neither could get the other out of their mind. Confessing this to each other, they decided to try counseling, which they had never done before. Months later changes began to occur and the former husband and wife decided to try again. This time they brought new communication skills into their marriage that they had learned during therapy.

. . . .

We will make it this time, for we have worked hard to become a team.

Stub and Doris' marriage was okay — not perfect, just okay. It wasn't until 17 years after they were married that Doris had an inkling of what their problem had been.

Stub felt his wife had always been a bit too reserved in bed. He was always the initiator and while she was willing, it was never with much enthusiasm. One evening they were watching a TV movie of the week about incest. Doris began to cry. The movie touched a nerve that she didn't even know she had. Memories suddenly surfaced and Doris realized that she had been sexually abused as a young child.

Long-term therapy unlocked old memories and helped Doris work on years of keeping her secret buried. Slowly, sometimes painfully, she gained understanding of her fears and her life began to improve.

. . . .

It is not easy to admit I was the victim of incest but I am proud I have gone for help.

There is a pattern many of us follow when we marry. Usually, it begins with a small apartment while we finish school or save money. Then children and, eventually, we may be able to buy a home, picket fence and all. Under no circumstances did we anticipate that either of our parents would live with us. This happens on occasion, due to financial constraints or health problems.

It takes two committed people and a strong marriage to live under the same roof with parents. People do it successfully all the time. By setting rules, talking out problems instead of letting resentments build and finding time to be alone, more than two generations can successfully live together.

We feel it is a wonderful advantage to our children and to us to have their grandparents living here. We are happy to share our home.

One of the most difficult situations we can get into is when we have total disapproval from our parents about something we want to do.

Such is the case when a parent forbids an adult child to marry the person he or she is in love with, especially when it is because he or she is not of the same religion. In some cases, as in the Orthodox Jewish religion, the child is mourned as if dead. In other families, the child is told, "Don't come to us if you have problems — we never want to see you again."

Having the strength to move forward on un-popular convictions is brave and scary. Committed to their love and the promise their lives hold together, adult children do what they must, regardless of their parents' threats.

. . . .

I am sorry my parents do not approve of my marriage but we have chosen each other and will proudly stay together.

John was an up-and-coming insurance executive. He and his bride, Ursula, each worked hard at their jobs and worked equally hard to insure their marriage would be a success. They were very much in love — it was plain for anyone to see.

One day, Ursula arrived home to find John curled up in bed, unresponsive. After he was hospitalized, the doctor told her about John's sudden mental illness. He said it would be hard and might take months or even years for her husband to recover.

Times were hard. Eventually John began to respond to treatment and was able to come home. Medication helped, though he had occasional relapses. Life was not the same, but together they would make it through.

. . . .

*I believe in my vows, ". . . in sickness
and in health," and will stand
by my husband always.*

It happens to the best of families. For some reason, a person turns to addictive substances. Some people can hide their addiction for a while. Others completely fall apart.

LaDonna was using crack. Her husband, Jim, knew as well as her co-workers and family. They decided to stage an intervention to confront her with their concerns. LaDonna cried and denied it all but her loved ones and close friends wouldn't back down. In the end, she agreed to go into a treatment program.

I feel lucky to have people around me who love me and are willing to stay with me while I recover.

When two people marry who have been married before and one or both has children, a step-family is created. This situation can be fraught with problems or may turn out relatively easy to handle.

A lot depends upon the ages of the children. If they are very young, they are most likely to be accepting of their new stepmom or stepdad. The older they are, the more difficult the situation can become.

Remarriage with children is never easy but if all the adults cooperate — and all stand united in the common cause of effective child-rearing, love and discipline, then with time, patience and effort, a new family will emerge.

. . . .

I am committed to helping
my children and my new spouse
feel comfortable as a family.

During our childhood years our parents, teachers and other relatives all contributed to how we think about ourselves today.

Strong, handsome, beautiful, intelligent — all words which build image. Stupid, ugly, worthless, no-good, unwanted — all destroyers. If, in our relationships, we continue to be knocked down emotionally, we will feel worthless. Sadly, we may live our entire lives without knowing our true self-worth.

Miraculously, people do change. They get out of abusive, addictive or enabling situations and begin a quest for recovery. There is always hope. It is never too late to change.

From this day forth I will remember that I am a worthy person.

One of the hardest emotions to let ourselves feel is that of being vulnerable. When we are upset, needy, or disappointed, it may be very hard for us to let anyone else know.

Bluff and bravado is what we used to call it — the "swaggering cowboy" image. Everything is cool and we have it under control. We all know people who answer, "I'm just fine," even when it is apparent they are not.

Allowing ourselves to admit vulnerability, to let ourselves accept help, to express our own feelings and to be receptive to being loved unconditionally may be a new and difficult experience but when we do, we discover a whole new world.

Once I let myself admit I was feeling vulnerable, it became easier to ask for what I needed.

Years ago, Theresa Brewer used to sing, "Little Things Mean A Lot." That song had a large impact on those who finally realized that there is more to love than just providing support and a home.

People rarely complain when they love each other, have a good life together, healthy children and a nice place to live. Yet something they are not aware of may be missing from their marriage.

There is a special feeling when the one you love gives you a small gift or does a chore you dread doing without being asked. It is the little things, the daily hugs and kisses or remembering to say "I love you" that show us we are cherished.

. . . .

Giving small gifts and doing things for each other that have special meaning make our strong relationship even stronger.

As parents, these days we are accused of pushing our children too fast. Gone are the quiet evenings of Kick the Can and playing tag in the backyard. Gone also are catching fireflies and letting them go.

In our video-oriented, television and high-achieving computer society, we may have gone overboard the other way. It seems as if we spend our days playing catch-up. We rarely sit down for home-cooked meals anymore. Instead, we go to the drive-through and eat in the car on the way to our next stop.

We can't change society, but we can allow ourselves to slow down. We need to smell the roses and catch fireflies, and so do our children. A fast-paced life is okay sometimes, but not all the time.

. . . .

In order to accomplish what I must, I owe myself some slower-paced days to refuel my spiritual energy.

133

Spirituality

When questioned about their spirituality, some people responded, "Oh, I'm not very religious. I rarely go to church." Spirituality is not a topic we think about often.

Currently unmarried we find ourselves giving thought as to how we want to live our lives. Day by day, we begin to develop a new lifestyle. Rather than mourn our lost love, we begin to look forward to awakening each morning to see what our day has in store for us.

Our sense of spirituality is awakening. Eager to face the day, we hear birds outside our window, notice that the day is sunny and that we feel sunny, also. We begin to reconnect with the world around us.

. . . .

As my soul awakens, I am enriched by the world around me and it is mine to enjoy.

It seems natural that some of us, as we begin to date, may look for a person opposite from the one we've just divorced. This is fine, especially if we have taken the time to get over our past relationship.

A very young woman may find herself dating a much older man, old enough to be her father. While an older woman might find she is happiest with a man young enough to be her son.

As long as we are not rebounding and have allowed ourselves time to heal, we have the right to choose our new partner. True love, respect and a strong commitment are what really matter.

. . . .

Now that I am free to choose a
new mate, I vow not to make
the same mistakes again.

The Shunned Parent

When a marriage dissolves, most couples try to maintain a sense of respect and equilibrium around their children. When this is destroyed, when one parent speaks negatively about the other, the children become confused as to what the truth really is or who to believe.

The shunned parent carries a terrible burden. Having done nothing wrong, that person can only continue to demonstrate love and affection for the children and hope that one day they will realize the truth.

As time passes, the parent who has been verbally abused by the other in front of the children, strives to live an honorable life, perhaps moves into a new relationship and gets on with a new life.

. . . .

Each day I will think positive thoughts
about my children, about how much
I will always love them.

We were always taught, as children, to forgive and forget. When teased by a best friend or hit by one of our siblings, our parents always encouraged us to "shake hands and make up."

Years of hurt feelings have accumulated by the time some of us decide we no longer can stay married. We remember our parents' admonitions and feel as though we need to "shake hands," to apologize for the marriage not working.

Occasionally we can't forgive and we don't want to have anything to do with our ex. It is best then to let ourselves forget without forgiving. Some things just can't be forgiven.

By allowing myself to forget the pain caused in my relationship, I give myself the gift of freedom to begin again.

Why is it common for two people raised in highly dysfunctional families to find each other and fall in love? They each must serve some sort of need for the other.

Dysfunctional behavior may go on throughout a marriage, both partners enabling co-dependency, or giving into the addiction.

Once in a while one partner realizes that they are in a bad situation and instead of pulling away, they work together toward recovery. Two people, once dysfunctional, struggle to be a functional couple. Not easy but possible.

It was frightening at first to give up old patterns of behavior. Now I am so happy that I did.

Once they were a happy all-American family. Mom, Dad, two kids, two dogs, one cat and some goldfish. They were the envy of everyone in their neighborhood.

Even all-American families occasionally run into personal problems. In this particular case, the husband and wife were growing apart. Rarely did they have a good conversation. They just lived in the same house drifting further and further from intimacy and commitment. They mutually separated.

When two people respect and care for each other, they try to formulate a good plan for their children. The less disruption they feel, the better it will be for all concerned.

....

I can rise to the challenge of being a divorced parent. I did not divorce my children.

"Look at me when I am talking to you!" We all remember our parents saying this to us. We looked but often didn't listen.

Learning to listen without interrupting, really listen to another person, is a skill that doesn't come automatically with age. Some of us never learn good listening skills.

When a marriage starts to flounder, if the couple cares enough to look at their problems, they will be surprised to find that they never really hear what the other one is saying. It isn't until we learn to pay close attention, to answer reflectively, that we begin to listen well.

. . . .

I now hear what is being told to me;
I have finally learned to listen.

There are unwritten rules in many families. For example they only want to hear about successes. We keep our own counsel when we fail.

Children and adults who succeed have many good tales to tell. The others feel like failures all the time. They bring no glory to their family, they reason, and therefore are not made to feel worthwhile.

A close family, whose members care about one another, shares both the good and bad in life. They stand behind one another, continue to believe in each other and support the decisions each person makes.

. . . .

In our family we love each other even if there are problems to deal with.

One problem with being newly divorced or separated is living alone through the times we used to spend together.

It has been said that a new widow or widower should not make any major decisions for one year. This is also true for divorce. Even if we get back into the swing of things socially, sad feelings still emerge as our anniversary rolls around and we remember the way we celebrated birthdays and holidays together.

Going through a whole year of "firsts" alone helps us grieve and allows us to "close out" our relationship. After a year of "firsts," we can move on more easily.

. . . .

Now that the first year is over,
I feel free to begin anew.

Ignoring our need to eat well-balanced meals, some of us try to get by with cold cereal, cookies, coffee with toast and fast-food. We may even splurge once in a while and order a pizza.

Ignoring our need to exercise, we become couch potatoes, watching television all evening. Our daily life pattern has been shattered by divorce . . . we don't know how to take care of ourselves.

We must allow ourselves to eat well and get enough sleep. Emotionally, we need to spend time with friends, new and old, and to talk about our problems. Exercise is important too, to be as healthy as possible.

. . . .

Because I am worthwhile, I can learn
to take care of my own physical
and emotional needs.

"You'll never be worth anything. You're no good." So many of us got this message, loud and clear, throughout our youth from parents as well as teachers.

Grades in school grew worse and so did our behavior. We believed those prophetic words and we stopped trying to be worth anything to anyone, least of all to ourselves.

Every now and again we get lucky, finding a person to marry who believes in us totally and in our ability to succeed. We find ourselves working hard to turn our lives around, to measure up to our spouse's total belief in our goodness and in our ability to do well.

. . . .

A positive prophecy, along with my mate's
unqualified love, has given me
a new lease on life.

First they were friends, participating in a number of college activities together. With so many interests in common and that special spark that creates a loving relationship, they decided to marry.

He was black, she was white. Both their parents liked them. Marriage, however, was another story. One evening they all sat down together for dinner. A long discussion ensued about the difficulties inherent in racially mixed marriages. They talked about prejudice, about having children.

With their parents' blessings and fully aware of the difficult and emotionally-charged situation, the couple began their married life together.

....

We entered our marriage aware of the problems, yet we are totally committed to each other.

For a while we may feel vacant emotionally. Closed off from our own feelings, we need some time to get over the finality of our divorce.

When we do allow ourselves to experience our feelings once again, many of us are surprised at how sad we feel, even if our marriages had actually turned sour. We are all taken by surprise when tears spring to our eyes for no apparent reason.

In order to take care of ourselves emotionally, we must lean right into our pain. Crying is good for us; it helps wash away sadness, frustration and even anger. We cry until we need to cry no more. No one has ever drowned in their own tears.

. . . .

Once I let myself cry,
I realized that I could
now move on with my life.

About 20 years ago Dr. Kubler-Ross gave us our most popular format for grief. We learned about the five steps of grieving: denial, bargaining, anger, depression and acceptance.

Why then, do we find ourselves grieving the end of a marriage? No one has died but, emotionally, we still need to close out the whole episode. Surprisingly, we may go through the same phases of grieving as though our spouse had died — except it was our marriage, our love, not our spouse who died.

By accepting the premise that we will grieve, and by allowing ourselves the right to work through each stage, we also give ourselves the freedom to enter a new relationship unencumbered.

The depth of my emotions surprises me.
Allowing myself to feel them lets me
shed my hurt feelings.

No matter how many people surround us when we celebrate our birthday and no matter how happy it is, the first time we have a birthday without our mate, memories crowd in of other birthdays we shared.

It gets easier as years pass but the good parts of our marriage, the wonderful times, don't disappear from our memories. Slowly, we replace old memories with new ones and often with a new person to love.

Eventually, remembering how we used to celebrate our birthdays and other special occasions became lessened by how we celebrate them now. New memories are sometimes even better. Happy Birthday to me!

I can choose what memories of our years together to cherish and which ones to cast aside.

Teenage girls often babysit for younger children. They enjoy making extra spending money, especially for clothes and makeup, and often like to pretend to be mothers. In many instances boys babysit as well, but few consciously practice fathering.

As newlyweds, we imagine that we will be perfect parents. In the grocery store, when we see a mother being unkind to her children or hear her say, "Because I said so, that's why!" we vow never to repeat that behavior.

Once we actually have children we try to parent patiently, with love and kindness, but it doesn't take very long for us to realize that it is not an easy job. No parent is perfect. All we can do is our very best.

My children will always know
they are loved unconditionally,
even when they misbehave.

They yelled so loudly that the neighbors could almost make out the words. Fighting, again and again, and always doing it in the same old way. Finally, both partners gave each other the cold shoulder and retreated to separate corners.

The silent treatment. Eventually, both the wife and her husband forgot what the fight was about. They never ended it and they never apologized.

Apologizing after a fight, instead of just letting it go away, is a more mature way of handling our problems. More importantly, we learn how to compromise. Fighting can be constructive if we use it as a tool to further communication.

· · · · · · · · · · · · · · · ·

Learning to fight fairly,
to compromise and apologize,
probably saved our marriage.

Both parents moved into new apartments. In this case, the mother has custody of the children. Finally, after months of adjusting to being divorced, she is ready to begin dating again.

Imagine the surprise when one or more of the children acts rudely toward a date. "I hate him!" one yells, while the other claims to have a bellyache. "Stay home, Mommy. I'm really sick."

The first few times we may actually stay home, since we are concerned parents. Finally, recognizing that the children are manipulating us, we over-ride their complaints and begin to date.

. . . .

I almost let my children run my life.
Then I remembered I am strong
and can set my own rules.

There is a pattern to all things. Bulbs blossom in springtime, gardens are harvested in summer. Humans have their seasons as well. A time for fertility and a time when we become barren.

These days, people don't hurry to begin their families. Far more career-oriented, we may wait for years after marriage to consider starting a family. The problem begins if we have been married for a long time, are getting divorced and never did take the time to have children.

Because their biological clocks are ticking away, some women rush into new relationships solely to have children. This works sometimes. Often a hurried marriage results in a hurried divorce.

....

Wanting children all my life, I made the right decision to have them now.

So in love. No one could feel love the way we do, we think, when we are first wed. Very physical, totally happy and understanding little about a truly adult relationship.

A year or two later the period comes when a real relationship begins to form, when companionship, commitment and common bonds take precedence. If, at this time, one partner depends completely upon the other for their sense of well-being, then the relationship is not balanced but co-dependent.

People who are co-dependent, who have come from dysfunctional families, need to get all their praise and comfort from an outside source, not from themselves. Unless we get or create what we need for ourselves, by ourselves, we will remain co-dependent.

. . . .

*I can get what I need by trusting myself
and my own instincts.*

Many years ago there was a movie called *Yours, Mine and Ours*. It was about a blended family with children from her marriage, his marriage and their marriage.

This was a wonderful premise for a movie but isn't quite so easy in real life. So much depends upon the ages of the children and the patience and devotion of the parents. Since they are so adaptable, younger children seem to do better than older ones. Teenagers may have the hardest time of all.

Blending a family is not an easy situation. It takes time, caring, persistence, Tough Love and genuine affection. Each child needs to feel valued and cherished, and to feel a part of the new functioning family unit.

. . . .

Sticking it out, struggling through the worst of times, has brought us all to the best of times.

We often characterize the person who has recently left a marriage as being "down," feeling really sad. This is not always the case. Some people feel just wonderful once they are no longer married.

Leaving a marriage can be cause for a celebration. Wanda threw a party to celebrate being single again. She and her friends laughed more in four hours than she and her husband had in four years.

Living alone, answering to no one's needs but her own and enjoying the privacy of her new life, she felt herself blossom and become again the happy person she once was.

. . . .

By celebrating my separateness,
my right to be who I am, I affirm my
ability to live a happy and contented life.

It is too bad so many of us are messed up permanently by our families of origin. And it is even sadder that once we recognize our problem, we still do nothing about it.

One of the hardest confessions to make is that we feel needy. Having become so used to squelching our own needs for either an addictive parent or spouse, we may not have learned to recognize our own feelings.

Learning to say "I need" and not to bury our feelings is no easy task. "I need to be hugged." "I need to stop enabling." And, yes, maybe even "I need to be separated from you and from our marriage."

One of my happiest moments occurred when I found the personal power to say "I need."

Out Of Balance

Balance is crucial to our survival. Balance between work and play, balance between meeting our own needs and meeting the needs of the people we love.

When life gets out of balance, when we tip too far in one direction and begin to ignore our own needs, we are sure to encounter some major difficulties.

Finding the balance between our emotions and our intellect, between what we feel and the way we say we feel, will help us. Intellectualizing when what we really want to do is to be hugged or to talk serves no one, least of all us.

. . . .

I am just learning to talk about my emotions and about what I am feeling. It feels good.

Many of us know what it is like to be trapped in an unhappy marriage: a recurring bad dream. Running. Running. But we can never get away.

There are so many reasons. Perhaps our spouse is kind but we just aren't committed anymore. Worrying that we wouldn't make it alone financially might be another. Or maybe, even though it is not a good marriage, we're afraid to leave what we know. Bad temper, addiction — the reasons are many.

Getting going, making that first move, is like trying to pull out of quicksand. Sucked back in by pleading, by unhappy children or even by our own guilt, we have a difficult time pulling away from our relationship.

. . . .

By garnering all my resolve, I can leave and make it on my own.

Unfinished business will, at some time in our lives, rise to haunt us. At that time we'll need to make it finished business, which we can then put away.

Unfinished business most likely developed when we were young. Since then we have carried all those hurts — either caused purposely or inadvertently by episodes from our childhood. Whether the issue was abuse or being ignored or whether we were loved too little, at some point all these issues will surface during adulthood.

When they do, we will need to deal with them in some way, such as professional therapy or a 12-Step program. Until we do, we will be incomplete adults.

. . . .

Forgiveness for my unfinished business will allow me to finish becoming an adult.

It is springtime. Daffodils bloom and many of us, depending on our religions, get ready to celebrate either Easter or Passover. As with other holidays, these springtime rituals allow us to both anticipate and celebrate the renewal of life.

We can easily meet other people who are also alone. Singles groups proliferate these days, covering interests in many areas, from sports to religion to travel or music.

If we have no one to spend holidays with, many churches and synagogues offer community services to be shared by all who wish to participate. By joining with others we reach out — and they will extend their hands to us.

All I need to do is reach out to people to share with. There are many who are also alone.

A trip to the bookstore these days yields hundreds of self-help books. Available on subjects from Alcoholics Anonymous to zodiac signs, books offering ways to grow surround us.

Many contain valuable information but the truth is that books are only half the answer. First we read and then we need to figure out what to do with our new-found knowledge — how to make it work for us.

Going the extra step and applying what we have learned to our real-life situation is not easy. The first step is always the hardest.

. . . .

Just reading by itself will not suffice.
I can plan my own future
and take positive action.

When two people who have been in love decide to separate, neither really anticipates what a vacuum will be created in our lives. The clock ticks very slowly as we begin to adjust.

Even if it is temporary, we need to add structure to our days, to our lives as they are right now. The plans we make early on may not be the same as the ones we adopt later.

Recognizing that adjustment to marital breakup comes slowly, we try hard to give our days a pattern, to keep them from being aimless.

I need to make a brand new life plan before I can abandon the old one.

Marriage starts out so exciting. We have a whole new life to face together. It ends with one or both of us completely disenchanted with the other and even with the idea of being married.

We separate and subsequently divorce, yet little do we realize how much we have given up, how much will change now in our lives. We lose the companionship and partnership of our best friend. Gone is the security, both emotional and financial, we had during our marriage. And often, but not always, we lose our self-confidence now that we are alone.

By admitting disenchantment with my marriage, I can bravely face my future.

It is a common enough situation. Separated now, we start to carve out a new niche for ourselves. Socially we are just starting to feel comfortable again. Dating a bit, going out with our other unmarried friends, life is definitely taking a turn for the better.

And then it happens. It is like waiting for the other shoe to drop. We get a phone call, often tearful: "Honey, I've made a terrible mistake. I don't want to get a divorce. Please, can we get together again?"

As tempted as we may be to go back to some form of security, back to what we know and whom we know, it takes a great deal of personal fortitude to say no. And with that single word, we have freed ourselves.

. . . .

In taking a stand and saying no,
I have moved one step closer to building
a new life on my own.

After a heart attack, wired to the monitor, patients watch the green blips move across the screen. As frightened as they feel, each blip reassures them that they are still alive, still vital.

A divorce can also be considered a blip on the screen of our lives — not following the normal pattern we expected our adulthood to take. Like the ocean, we also have an ebb and flow as part of the pattern of life, yet we always expect that our waves will smooth out and go back to their original source of energy.

Since we don't wish to return to our marriages, we can, instead, return to the source of our strength, our Higher Power, to guide us to a smooth new pathway.

. . . .

My Higher Power has given me the strength and the right to make choices about how I will design my life.

The happiness of a marriage largely depends upon how it fulfills our expectations. If we have low expectations, food, clothing and the occasional meeting of our sexual needs, we'll be happy so long as those needs are satisfied.

When partners in a marriage never discuss their expectations of one another, they may both be disappointed at the results. Even worse is when they did discuss it and one partner does not honor the agreement or chooses to stop trying.

In order for a troubled marriage to survive, we eventually will need to redefine our expectations and to commit ourselves to each other once again. We can never stop working on a relationship.

. . . .

*While one person alone cannot hold
a marriage together, two people
who work on it can.*

These are famous last words, heard by most of us at one time or another during a relationship. "Look, dear, I just have to get it out of my system. I can quit whenever I want to, I promise."

It matters little whether the promise is to quit gambling, an affair or physical or substance abuse. Because we are in love, we do believe the promise, over and over. We continue to have faith that our partner, our best friend, will make the right choice, the good choice.

Ultimately, we recognize that the choice is ours, not theirs. To stay and continue being an enabler. Or to leave if they don't keep their promise.

. . . .

My own famous last words are,
"I promise myself I will no longer
be co-dependent — an enabler."
I owe that to myself.

What a sinking feeling we had when one or both of our parents called us into the living room with a stern voice and said "Get in here! We need to talk." Uh, oh. Trouble.

Nowadays we use those same words but we use them to assist in our relationships. They may herald trouble on the horizon or perhaps just a problem which needs solving. "We need to talk" is not always a call to arms.

Instead, we can use our ability to communicate to talk about our pressing needs. Learning to say "It hurts me when" or "I need you to listen to me" or "Please hug me" can be marriage savers. No longer should we fear talking seriously to the one we love.

. . . .

Our ability to talk, really talk, to each other has helped our marriage survive.

While our marriage is thriving and whole, we stand by each other, supportive and loving. When we can no longer find solutions to solve a growing list of problems, the time may have come to end it.

It is not an easy decision to get divorced. Even more difficult is when our church, our family or our community completely disapproves of our action.

Standing by our decision becomes more and more difficult as we are censored by those who disagree. No matter who disagrees with us, no matter what group is angry, we stand firmly by our decision.

. . . .

It hurts me that people don't approve of my divorce but I must do what is best for me.

A Different Love

For many of us, the words "true love" conjure up roses, park benches and a special someone to love. Of course, most of us love our children and our parents as well.

These days, admitting to any other kind of love strikes our homophobic society as either abnormal or a frank confession of homosexuality. Paranoia reigns, quite unreasonably, in that arena right now.

One experience we can enjoy, even more now that we are no longer married, is to love our closest friends dearly but in a totally non-intimate way. It is often our friends who support us through the roughest times, who stand by our side when we laugh and cry.

. . . .

*The freedom to love my friends,
and the fact that I have friends,
warms my heart daily.*

We often hear recently divorced friends say emphatically, "Well, that's finally over. I will never get married again as long as I live!" While uttered sincerely, this statement may or may not turn out to be true.

Suffering hurt feelings and damaged esteem is a plight shared commonly among the "again single" group. It may take a very long time — and may never happen — until we are ready to risk playing the dating game.

Once we do begin, our readiness to form another love alliance grows. Pass the salt and pepper — we may have to eat our words! Never is a very long time.

. . . .

While I do not miss my former spouse,
I do miss being married. I trust myself
enough now to fall in love again.

Entitlement — a word fraught with possibilities. Just because we have been hurt emotionally by the ending of our relationship doesn't give us a reason not to use good judgment when taking care of ourselves.

Going to excess in any area is more than just indulgence; it is often over-indulgence. "I'm entitled to eat all this chocolate," we rationalize or to buy ourselves a new wardrobe or to order that new red convertible. "After all, I really did suffer," we tell ourselves soothingly.

Negative emotions and a poor sense of self-worth cannot be made to feel better by indulging our every desire. Instead, we must evaluate our needs and deal with them in a reasonable fashion.

. . . .

What I am entitled to is to feel my full range of emotions and to be happy.

Endings can be very hard. We'll probably make several false starts before we can really let ourselves finish the relationship.

As we begin anew, unmarried, we may be uncertain of what role we played in the failure of our marriage. Not until we identify our problem areas, not until we deal with those troublesome behaviors, can we let go of old baggage. There isn't much sense in loading a luggage cart that is already full.

Having a sense of direction to our lives as well as setting some new goals will allow us to begin the slow and uncertain journey that will meander through the rest of our lives.

. . . .

I can enter a new relationship unfettered once I have let go of my old problems.

Once any relationship is over, whether it is a marriage, a love affair or even a relationship with one of our parents, there is no going back to the way things were before.

There is also no way to re-enter our marriage expecting it to be entirely changed. We can't take back the bitter words or withdraw the hurt caused by an escalating battle. We know this intellectually but we still have to try to make it all right again.

There is no going back. By facing our own role in the marital breakup or in the failure of any old relationship, we can begin to move on with our lives.

. . . .

Once I face the fact that I caused
some of my own troubles,
I can grant myself forgiveness.

Now time hangs so heavily on our hands —
time that used to be filled with meeting our
family's needs, listening to chattering children
at the dinner table or cuddling together on the
sofa and watching television.

This extra time looms large. It may leave us
anxious and drives home how alone we feel.
We just can't hurry our healing process.

By giving ourselves the time and space we
need to heal, we also put distance between the
event and our future. Slowly, we start to make
new plans.

. . . .

*I was frightened at first by so much free
time, by my loneliness. Now I see it as
an ally to my healing process.*

Children may do everything in their power to break up new relationships, to thwart any new romance. Siblings who often bicker may shock us with their unity now that we are beginning to date.

All we want is the right to date and, perhaps one day, to become involved again. All they want is for their parents to get back together. If that is not possible, then they want to keep the parent with custody all to themselves.

We can be quite torn apart between our children's needs and our own. As long as we are fair and honest with our children and take the time to listen to their needs, our need for adult companionship can and should be the ultimate winner.

. . . .

My children are a part of life, but not my whole life. They cannot dictate how I meet my needs.

Hugh couldn't deny it any longer. His parents, no matter how much he loved them and tried to be a good boy, were really cruel to him. Of all the four kids, he was the one who always got the beating, always got the nasty looks and got knocked around.

When he was 35, Hugh hit his 12-year-old daughter. It was the first time, and as he sat crying on her bed, apologizing, he vowed it would be the last. Hugging his crying daughter he made himself a promise to get help.

Beginning therapy was hard. Telling the truth about his childhood was even harder. But soon, Hugh began to reach his "child within" and began to parent himself. Before long, Hugh realized he was finally, at 35, growing up.

. . . .

I am finally learning to take care of my own emotional needs, so that I can better take care of my family.

It isn't an easy task to learn to accept ourselves as we are. It is harder still to learn to love ourselves, faults and all. This task may seem monumental after the breakup of our marriage.

There are several things we can do to help ourselves move along to a healthier place. First, we need to accept who we are and not blame ourselves now that our relationship has failed. It also helps to work on letting go of the love we used to feel for someone else and instead try to give it to ourselves.

Filling our emotional and physical needs, pampering ourselves until we feel better, and accepting that the relationship is over and that we need to move on, all will help us make our personal adjustment.

. . . .

I can look to myself, my close friends
and my God to help me through
this rough time in my life.

In every relationship there are both good and bad days — which extend into good and bad weeks. Our need to "make it right," to settle our disputes, pushes out most thoughts of discontent.

Regardless of what we are fighting about, we will always do better if we wait to use our interpersonal communication skills until the moment is right.

Poor timing in conversation literally kills a lot of relationships. Having a heart-to-heart talk while dinner is burning or the income tax forms are being filled out is asking for disaster. It is not just talking but finding the right time to talk that is equally important.

. . . .

Weighing what I say and when I say it
helps me remember to be honest
yet gentle with my words.

Our sense of self-worth can become very low, especially when we have decided to break up with someone we have been involved with for a long time.

The people who surround us after we have ended our relationship — close friends, co-workers, family members — may be disgruntled with the finality of the move. This is especially true if they really liked our partner. They become angry that we ended it.

Because we need approval so desperately, we may be tempted to change our minds, just to please the people we care so much about. When we recognize what we have considered doing just for approval, we are appalled.

. . . .

I want to please those who love me but
I owe it to myself to please me first.

From the time we were young, how people thought of us always helped dictate how we thought and felt about ourselves. When we decide to separate, positive expressions from others give us strong support as we make our decision.

We generally know how to meet basic physical needs — food, comfort, warmth and shelter. Socially we may sometimes conflict and not find the acceptance and confirmation we crave.

Deciding to leave often fills a deeper need than approval from others — the need to feed our ego. When we feel comfortable about ourselves and about our decision to leave, we will do just fine.

. . . .

More than support from my family
when I leave my marriage,
I need support from myself.

It is so hard to take criticism constructively. Old feelings from childhood creep back as we remember that dreadful teacher who criticized us in front of our whole classroom.

Criticism can be destructive or constructive. Continual negative criticism most assuredly will cause a relationship to break down. It is especially difficult to be criticized by someone we love.

Designed to enhance performance or behavior, creative constructive criticism often begins with praise and then moves on to the area that needs work. It is far easier to accept criticism when we get some positive strokes.

. . . .

I am grateful to those people who offer me constructive suggestions. These help me not to repeat the behaviors which contributed to the failure of my marriage.

Each of us has our own value system; the basic concepts of good and bad were taught to us as children. Ending our commitment to the person we vowed to spend our life with goes against our basic principles.

What we want to believe in, right or wrong, makes up our belief system. As youngsters, we found that the Tooth Fairy, Santa Claus and Jack Frost fit soundly into our belief system. Breaking up a marriage does not.

Attitudes, however, are of deepest importance to us. These include intense values we hold near and dear. We incorporate into them our belief that even if we failed at one relationship, we can keep a positive attitude and succeed in another relationship.

. . . .

I strongly believe in myself
and in my personal power to
adjust to changes in my life.

Neither here nor there — that is how we feel when we are in the process of being separated. As each area of contention is being negotiated, we might find ourselves wistful and somber about our breakup.

Separation can be a painful and confusing time of life. Still unclear as to whether we have made the right decision, yet eagerly awaiting the actual dissolution, we teeter back and forth with our emotions.

By wanting and needing it to be over, as we move toward the day we sign the papers, we feel strongly that we have made the right decision and are no longer ambivalent.

. . . .

The time it took to complete the
divorce process gave me the time
I needed to begin healing.

He wistfulllly remembered the last Fourth of July. It was one of their all-time great family picnics. None of the kids had bickered, the weather was gorgeous and they went on a long walk around the lake.

When his wife decided she no longer wanted to be married — that she suddenly needed to live on a religious commune — a long, hard custody fight ensued. Somehow she got custody.

Now he was alone, 3,000 miles from his children. He rarely had the money or vacation time to see them but he could talk to them by phone. His lifestyle had certainly changed and there was little he could do about it.

· · · · · · · · · · · · · · · · ·

Alone, I must struggle daily to learn
to trust and love again.

My Fault

Grounded for the weekend, working hard on a large puzzle in his room, Andrew heard his parents fighting in their bedroom. He had never heard them fight like this before.

At 11, Andrew knew he had really disappointed his folks when he skipped school with Johnny that day. He wondered if they were fighting about him.

A few days later, his parents sat both of their children down and announced they were separating and, most likely, would get a divorce. Deep inside, Andrew felt it was all his fault but he couldn't say the words. He became a small child carrying a terrible burden.

. . . .

Even though we got a divorce, I must be clear with my children that they were in no way responsible.

There once was a couple who appeared to have "the perfect marriage." They still kissed in public, held hands and they never fought.

The children of this very special couple entered their own marriages with a very distorted view of what a marriage was really like. The first time their daughter fought with her new husband, she thought their marriage was destined to fail.

Fighting! Her parents had never fought. Crying, she called home. "You and Daddy never fought. I'm a failure at marriage!"

"Nonsense, dear," her mother replied, "we fought all the time, just never in front of you children." Relieved, the daughter felt better.

. . . .

Parents who never have words in front of their children give them an unfair perspective on the reality of living together.

One of the most important facets to the survival of a long-term relationship is our ability to have close interpersonal communication. This means developing good listening skills and giving our full attention to the conversation at hand.

There is one area, however, that may be ignored as too personal or embarrassing — expressing sexual need. Assuming we know automatically what our partner needs, either by inference or by unspoken signals, indicates that neither of us really knows how to satisfy the other.

Learning to say, "I need . . . I don't like it if . . . Please do that again," or "It feels so good" are important phrases which will enhance our life together in all areas, including our sexual needs.

. . . .

By listening to each other we can optimize all facets of our life together.

Remember sitting under a tree in summertime with a friend, slowly pulling petals from a daisy and chanting, "He loves me, he loves me not"? By the time we finally figured out we should start with "He loves me not," we were too old to play the game.

If only life were so easy now. Should we stay in a problem marriage or not? Some parts are very good, others quite horrible. It is the good part we can't let go of so easily.

Sitting down with pen and paper and drawing up a pro and con chart may help us make up our mind. Using positive and negative sentences such as, "It makes me angry when he . . ." "I feel happy when . . ." really helps us take a good look at how our marriage functions.

....

Surprisingly, my list convinced me to stay.
We will get some help to deal
with our marriage.

There is no such thing as a perfect parent. There may be days when we feel perfect but those days are few and far between.

We find our own equilibrium as new parents and, further, we slowly identify each other's areas of strength and weakness. In this way we complement the other's parenting skills.

When one of us undermines parental authority, especially in front of the children or other family members, we find we have made a grave error in judgment. Parenting battles are for private times. In this way we both save face and become more unified as parents.

. . . .

*We can undermine each other or stand
united as parents. I choose unity.*

"We agree then. We'll try a six-week separation." Emotionless words, uttered in business-like tones, so neither of us gives in to the sadness of the moment. Separation was not something we planned.

A separation can actually be a good time, although we may not see it at first. It can be used as a time for personal growth and decision-making. Getting to know ourselves again, in a separated status, can really be an eye-opener.

When the six weeks are up, we sit down once again to talk. In some instances, it is really over. In others, during the time we have spent apart, how important we are to each other and how much love we share become readily apparent.

. . . .

The thinking time afforded by my
separation helped me understand how
important we are to each other.

The Wimbledon tennis championships were on again. "Wow! Look at that! Becker really set his opponent up."

"Yeah," Asa agreed, "set him up to smash him down, right?"

Innocent enough, this situation happens in our own homes. A husband says, "Which tie should I wear, honey — brown or green?"

"Oh," she answers, "I think the green one looks much better."

"Darn!" he spouts, "I knew you'd say that. I hate that green tie!"

Too often we expect and allow this behavior as part and parcel of being married. Some of us finally realize we're being set up as surely as Boris Becker's opponent, so we stop being a participant in the game. "Make your own decision, dear. You're the one who has to wear the tie."

....

By bowing out,
I choose to let both of us win.

Eureka! The chemistry is right, the circumstances are great and the person we have fallen in love with even loves us back.

Months later, still getting along famously and having spent countless hours together, the two families meet and get along like old friends. We know where our relationship is headed and we can't wait.

But we do. And wait. And wait. A long talk becomes inevitable. At which time we are told, "I love you so much. It's just that I'm not ready to make a commitment yet. I may never be ready." We have become involved with a person who has stolen our heart and then has broken it in two.

. . . .

Time lost by unrequited love
cannot be regained. I shall
struggle to heal myself.

When we promised to spend our lives together, loving and caring for one another, we really promised always to be there, even during the hard times.

In the normal course of a relationship there will be disagreements and even some fights, but basically, we revere one another and always try to stay aware of our loved one's feelings.

Once in a while, often in public, we embarrass our partner — either intentionally or completely inadvertently. Seeing the hurt it has caused, we promise never to do it again. The hurt feelings we created were not worth the reaction they caused.

. . . .

I promise never to knowingly
embarrass the one I love.

Getting older, we pass from one stage of life to another, often marrying and having children. This is the best time of our lives, we say, regardless of what stage we are in.

We have many years to earn money, to succeed, to acquire everything we want. We consider ourselves lucky if our marriage is a happy one, if we are in a profession we enjoy, if our children "do us proud."

Somewhere near 40 or 45, as we ponder our lives, we know we've finally matured. We realize now that it is not our net worth or who we know that matters at all. Real success in life comes from feeling good about ourselves, doing for others and working, at least in some small way, to improve the human condition.

. . . .

There is more to my life than making money.
I feel good when I help other people.

Leaving a marriage, especially one that survived a long time, is an emotionally-fraught situation. Even under the worst of conditions, there is a heart-wrenching moment when we realize it is truly over.

Taking the time to listen, to sympathize and to try to understand our decision, our close friends further endear themselves when they comment, "This has been really hard for you. What are your plans? Are you going to be all right?"

True friends, not the fair-weather variety, are with us all the way, through good and bad times. Whether they approve of our decision or not, they don't make value judgments but instead support us as we move through the hard process of adjustment.

. . . .

As each day passes I cherish my friends
even more for caring about me
and for showing it.

Religious retreats and marriage encounters proliferate these days. During the difficult time we are deciding whether or not to end our marriage, we may choose to participate in one of these retreats.

Hopefully we will gain heightened awareness of how our interpersonal problems have contributed to the trouble in our relationship. We may even be able to save our marriage. We also may learn why we developed such problems in the first place.

Now that we are home, perhaps we can incorporate what we have learned into the everyday trappings of our lives and use the knowledge to help us formulate a new life plan.

. . . .

Painful as it is to dig deep and learn about myself, I will reap the benefits many times over.

We have, as a nation, learned new sexual habits. Sexually transmitted diseases have reached epidemic proportions, often causing infertility or death.

If we suspect our husband or wife is having an extra-marital affair, it is not too difficult to put the pieces of the puzzle together. A small part of us really doesn't want to know; the mature part knows we must, for our own safety.

The final blow may occur when we discover that proper birth control has not been used, both to prevent pregnancy and to prevent disease. If we cannot condone promiscuity nor forgive our partner, we have no choice but to end our marriage.

My mate's promiscuous behavior destroyed my trust and I had no choice but to separate.

There are courses to teach us auto repair,
how to prepare taxes and even yoga. The one
course we need most, parenting, is rarely available.

Unfortunately, we suddenly get on-the-job
training, want it or not. Physically caring for an
infant can be more exhausting than running a
26K race. At least with a marathon, we have
time to train!

As unprepared as we are, we learn together,
bringing to parenthood experience passed on
by our own parents. We hone our skills as years
go by and develop a silent promise never to
criticize parenting skills in front of the children.

. . . .

*The support we show each other as
we parent is only a fraction of our
overall support for each other.*

We all do it. "Just ten more mintues," we mutter, as we prepare to slam the snooze alarm one more time. Procrastination becomes a way of life — almost an art-form for some.

Some continually put off making important decisions, such as whether to put money down on a house, to have children or not or, in the worst case, whether or not to separate. We are actually announcing our decision by making no decision at all.

In love with a procrastinator, one who is never on time and rarely completes work, we may actually need to decide if we can tolerate that behavior for years to come. And we will decide — soon!

. . . .

I accept that I cannot change my beloved's procrastinating behavior.

Passing by the bathroom mirror, we stop, throw back our shoulders and look at our image. "Hmm. When did I get those gray hairs?" We all change — it is a normal and expected part of our lives.

Change can be quite positive, heralding many exciting days to come. We anticipate children, moving to a larger living space and even retirement. We expect to change as the years pass by.

In order to stay together as a happily married couple, we must both change in similar or other complimentary ways over the years. It won't always be equal but the important message is never to become complacent or stagnant.

. . . .

Over the years we have both changed and
we grow more in love and more
committed to each other.

"You're the man in the family now" is a phrase often told to the oldest son by his well-meaning, newly divorced mother. "I'll be depending on you."

This puts an undue burden on the older child, since he already may feel somewhat responsible for his mother's well-being. If the child feels sad, the mother may feel sad, too.

Children need to be children and will usually accept added responsibilities as they mature. In the presence of divorce, children may be more responsible than in a two-parent family. Confusion may reign if the child is getting mixed messages and no longer has a clearly defined role.

....

Expecting my child to fill an adult's shoes is really an injustice. I will let my children be children.

Abused again but never knowing what we have done to deserve it, we feel demoralized. Still, we hang on to our marriage for those few moments when it works and for the inevitable apology we know is forthcoming. Secretly, we believe that the abuse will end, that our lot will improve.

Because we spend our lives trying to please our partner and because it has become a habit to let ourselves be beaten down, we have totally lost our sense of self-esteem.

"I'm really sorry. I promise I'll never hit you again. You know how much I love you." We need to believe, so we accept the apology as genuine. Grasping at straws, at even a tiny amount of praise, we let it slide until the next awful attack.

. . . .

I recognize my role as an enabler and will now gather the resources I need to leave.

Full of well-meaning advice, friends tell us what they think we need to know about being separated, about divorce and about what went wrong.

Actually, they may be loaded with excellent and very appropriate advice. We smile and nod, and maybe even occasionally listen but in reality their advice goes in one ear and out the other.

None of us ever learns anything, even as school children, until we are ready to learn. It takes time, perhaps years, to get to that place in our lives. Only then will we be ready to listen and to learn.

In the long haul, the only advice which matters to me is the advice I am ready to hear.

Most of us, with the passage of time and the gaining of wisdom, have become caring and responsible adults. Depending on what transpired in our childhood homes, some may have been "small adults" for many years, dealing with very large problems.

Now that our marital union has ended — the one thing we thought would be a constant in our adult lives — we tell ourselves that we will survive, that we will be okay even after being divorced.

In order to really begin healing, we will need to get in touch with the child who dwells within us — that person who may have been deprived of their childhood, who had to struggle too young with grown-up problems. It may take professional therapy to reach deep within, to search out and set free our deeply hidden child.

. . . .

Finding my child within scared me,
for to reach the child, I had to let go
of my adult inhibitions.

For years we buried our own needs to serve
the needs of others. Incredibly, we may have
been so busy with the constant demands on our
time that we actually thought we were happy.

Suddenly, having been divorced after so
many years, we have no one to please but ourselves. Time may hang heavily on our hands as
we struggle to figure out how to spend our
newly acquired spare time.

We can now freely begin the quest to discover ourselves. Hobbies and interests kept buried
by years of subservience can now be resurrec-
ted. We can take time to pamper ourselves, to
indulge in our own personal needs. This becomes a very special time for growth and self-
discovery.

. . . .

*I no longer feel guilty when taking
care of my own needs. I am able
to take care of myself.*

After a divorce, adjustment is a process we all must move through. We would like to hurry it up, to get going again but we can't push the passage of time.

Looking back over what that first year taught us, we marvel at how different our attitude was soon after the papers were signed, as opposed to how we felt months later. Not only do we go through a growth process we also move through the grieving process.

Naturally, in the first few weeks, we may not recognize that our adjustment has only just begun. This especially confuses us since we were eager to get out of a bad relationship. Only much later do we realize it takes work to get over a marriage.

. . . .

While I wanted to plunge into my new life,
I could not hurry my adjustment
to being divorced.

Drained of energy, tired from years of tiptoe-ing around the issues that caused us trouble, we may be extremely relieved now that our final divorce papers have come through.

"I kept waiting for my ex-spouse to come back through the door, to tell me I wasn't even any good at getting a divorce — that I've never been good at anything" is the lament of those who were married to people who could never be pleased, no matter how hard they tried.

A divorce may actually be a blessing in disguise, a release from years of trying to please a person who could never be pleased. It is time to please ourselves.

. . . .

Today is the beginning of my new life —
one which will never again include a
person who puts me down.

Living in a house with another person, even a husband or wife, means nothing if we don't both work together on our relationship. If we look back over the years, we realize how lonely we were even when we were married.

It took quite a while for Shirley to realize that even though her husband came home every evening, brought home a regular paycheck, didn't gamble and had never, to her knowledge, had an affair, they had almost nothing in common anymore.

Validation of who we are and how important we are to our partner is integral to our emotional survival in a marriage. Without validation, we become housemates, nothing more.

. . . .

Release from a person who never took time to validate me allows me to validate myself.

At first we accept the demand for us to justify our behavior as showing deep love and caring. Later, however, we take it for what it is — a rigid need by our loved one to control every aspect of our day.

Unless we personally have had to account to someone for our actions 24 hours a day, we can hardly understand living under such restrictions. From demanding details of lunch with friends to justification about the grocery bill, we are overwhelmed by this demanding behavior.

When we are alone after our breakup, it is time to give thought to how hard it was to live like that. We should not need to explain our behavior to anyone but ourselves.

. . . .

From this day forth I am free to be me.

From the time we were children, even in the most secure of families, we have had a fear of abandonment. Small children worry that their parents may not come home after an evening out. The older we get, the larger our fear of being abandoned becomes.

Ensconced in the security of our new marriage, we are not so frightened anymore since our loved one didn't leave us during the engagement and we are committed to a lifetime together.

If we fall out of love, as so many of us do, being abandoned may not be such a major issue. Instead, the major issue is to take care of ourselves and to survive on our own.

. . . .

I love myself enough to know I will be all right alone. I will not abandon myself.

Constant criticism can totally undermine our self-esteem. Often the criticism is concealed under the guise of humor. Loving someone is a powerful reason to try to ignore these words but they still hurt.

"Did you get a haircut, honey?" Naturally, we are immediately pleased that our new hair style has been noticed. "It looks like you stuck your head in a blender!" Bang! Shot in the heart again.

This is verbal abuse. Taught not to say anything if we had nothing nice to say, we find this to be confusing behavior. Leaving the room or announcing that you are hurt are two good ways to start to expressing our anger.

I have done nothing wrong and deserve no criticism.

They weren't even good together when they first started dating. Both Sam and Penny had the habit of constantly picking at each other, so even friends were uncomfortable being with them on double dates.

After high school graduation, they married, had a large flock of children and continued to pick at each other. It was their way of life. Then Sam started to drink. Things weren't the same after that. The money was used up by his addiction and Penny went out to do factory work.

Sam wasn't a mean drunk; he was just a drunk. Friends advised Penny to leave, to find a better life. "I can't. I know this life and I'd be scared to leave."

. . . .

The problems I know are better than the new ones I may encounter if I leave. I will stay in this marriage.

They were next-door neighbors, worshipped at the same church, went to the same school. They fell in love, married and enjoyed 25 wonderful years together.

After the initial years of struggling, their family business did very well. Then financial setbacks caused it to fail and the trouble began. Her husband, always jovial, friendly and warm, became morbidly depressed. His depression became so profound that even with extensive treatment, he just couldn't pull out of it.

Turning to the only job she had ever known, she became a housecleaner. Now the primary wage earner, they were barely making it. Sticking by her husband, never giving up hope, she bravely faced each day with a smile.

. . . .

There is only one goal now, to be healthy and happy again.

Battered husbands? "Well," we respond, "this is something new!" In fact, men have been battered for years but, until recently, were too proud to say anything about it for fear of destroying their image.

Some women are just not nice people. They pass for nice because they have learned all the appropriate social graces but, underneath, they can be quite cruel. This is not confined to people who are poor or even to people who were themselves battered.

Battering transcends race, religion and economic status. It may be physical; it may be emotional. Both are devastating. No one deserves to be battered.

Years of counseling helped me gain the confidence to leave. I can do it now.

"Mom, why are you and Daddy always so quiet around each other? Are you two angry?" This is a perfectly normal question for a child to ask.

Two people who have been together a long time develop certain ways of being with each other. One marvelous way to communicate is to be silent. Most people think that conversation means to talk but in the natural course of a conversation there are often pauses or quiet times.

"We are quiet because we don't have anything to say right now." But what she really means is that they have learned to talk between the lines and almost know what the other is thinking. Often, long-married couples begin to speak and words that are identical come out. Silence is golden.

. . . .

We do not have to talk out loud to communicate. Years of love and sharing create their own bond.

Family Feud

Fighting occurs in every family. Brothers and sisters do it and we even fight with our moms and our dads. It can become a big problem when we carry those childhood battles into adulthood.

If it matters to us that we get along with our family but we find ourselves stuck in old behaviors, it may be time to sit down and analyze why. No one really wants to have a fight each time they get together with family members.

Support groups, books and therapy are all available if we want to change. However, having done all those things, we may have to face the fact that the people who are fighting with us, our family members, may never change and don't want to.

. . . .

By freeing myself from the burden of my anger, I no longer feel the need to participate in family feuds.

The whole topic of child support after divorce is a very touchy one. Except in very special cases, when the custodial parent makes a great deal of money, child support should be provided.

There are people who feel that when their marriage is over, responsibility to their family ends. Some states have mandated payment of child support and can dock a paycheck as well as put the parent in jail. When the person either disappears or keeps promising but doesn't pay up, there will be no check in the mail.

The children now live with a parent who carries a new burden: how to keep them clothed and fed, and how to explain why their missing parent no longer seems to care about them.

. . . .

Regardless of my personal feelings,
I will not destroy my children's good
memories of their other parent.

Some people have the most difficult time making up their minds about anything. "Should I buy this suit or that one?" or "How about painting the house?" They agonize over every decision, large and small, pestering other people to solve their problems.

A person who is indecisive will always stay that way. When the issues get really serious, as when a marriage is failing, that type of indecision can be infuriating to other people involved. "I just don't know what to do. Should we get a divorce or not?"

When one of the partners loves the other and wants to stay married but the indecisive spouse who is discontented is "deciding," it can be a most difficult time. The very person you love keeps telling you they may leave.

....

I felt so rejected before my spouse finally
decided to leave. Now I understand
that it freed me as well.

There are support groups available for nearly every problem these days. Grieving. Dying. Coping with illness. Dieting. Addictions. Widowhood. Only in the past decade have groups sprung up for the newly divorced.

It is a scary time of life, even if we really wanted the divorce. We need to start again, especially socially, but our uncertainty over how to begin can be alleviated by attending groups specifically designed for other folks just like us.

Tentatively we attend, only to find out that everyone else there also felt uncertain at one time about beginning anew. Using the group as a springboard to other interests, we meet new friends, join in their activities and no longer feel lonely.

....

I have reassured myself that
I am still able to socialize and that
people are basically friendly.

Until we realize that we are not the only ones, that there are many other women being abused, we continue to allow it to happen. Knowing it is wrong, we stay for the security of a regular paycheck and the rare comfort offered in our marriage.

So beaten down that our self-image is virtually destroyed, we expect nothing better for ourselves. The story changes when our children are threatened or beaten. Knowing they could be hurt or even killed causes us to spring into immediate action.

Calling for help, dialing the police or 911, getting to a friend's house or a battered women's shelter is our most important move. More permanent plans can be made later.

. . . .

*I was terrified to leave but
did it to save my children. In doing so,
I also saved myself.*

"What poor table manners! If we get serious and get married, I can change all that!" Nearly every single person who has dated harbors a similar thought.

How naive we were to imagine that we could change another person's behavior. The only people who can change their behavior are themselves. What is considered to be problem behavior to one person may be perfectly acceptable to another.

Throughout life there will be reasons to change behavior. Situations arise with addiction, abuse and even with health habits that do need to be altered. Perhaps through the influence of a loved one and the care of professionals, change will occur.

. . . .

The only person's behavior I have a right to change is my own.

People stay in relationships for all sorts of reasons. Many of us, besides wanting to meet our basic needs, covet the whole idea of being married, of being a couple in a doubles world. Being married lends prestige to some, while being single can cause loss of esteem and make us feel "less than."

No marriage is ideal but some are less ideal than others. Spousal abuse is now a nationally recognized problem. Some spouses, knowing this, still choose to stay. Reasons vary, from "It only happens two or three times a year" to "Besides, we all have to take the bad with the good."

No one can tell others what is right for them. Each person has to decide what behaviors will be tolerated in a marriage.

. . . .

Once I garner enough emotional
strength, I can formulate plans which
allow me to leave.

When mired in the muck of a personal difficulty, at work, with the children or our partner, or even financial, we become bogged down with the very mechanics of facing each day.

First we have to figure out what is bothering us. Then, having identified the problem, we get ready to turn to outside help for a solution. This is not always necessary, for we carry deep within us the resources to solve many of our own difficulties.

Many times, when left to our own resources, we can solve our problem without any intervention from other sources. We need to give ourselves time to figure it out and have faith in ourselves that we can do it.

. . . .

*I can give myself the time I need to
creatively solve my own problems.*

Isn't it strange that when wé hear the term Superman, we think immediately of the movie, the character or the comic strip, but when Superwoman is mentioned, we automatically move to a completely different mindset?

We imagine a competent, tired, stressed woman trying to climb the corporate ladder and do it all. She often has a husband who is busy struggling up his own ladder and who may contribute little to the chores on the home front.

No single person, male or female, can do it all. We all need help, from spouses, from our children, and perhaps from outside people, too. In trying to reach the top, we lose sight, sometimes, of the importance of relationships, of hugging and of loving another human being.

. . . .

*Every day I will remind myself
of the importance of showing
love to my family.*

Recently, there has been a lot of press about the children of divorced parents. One book dealing exclusively with this topic has sold quite well.

Upon reading this book, we find that the children of divorced parents don't adjust as well as we thought. Many problems can surface in school and in socialization. This information throws a monkey wrench into the plans of people who are in the midst of getting a divorce. We don't mean to hurt our kids.

Some divorces are a complete necessity but others, the ones we can't decide about, may be delayed because of this news. An extra burden of guilt is not what we need when our marriage is failing.

. . . .

I will love and support my children,
both emotionally and financially after the
divorce but my happiness matters
as much as theirs.

How easy it would be, as we wade through old papers and mementos, to toss away all those papers and photographs that remind us of the time we were in love.

Too many of us do just that and are so sorry later. Love letters, small gifts, pictures and cards can really cut to the quick and we'd just as soon forget.

There may be a time when we need to look at those memorabilia or, more important, when our children will want to see them. Put them in a package, seal it up and pack them away. It is not easy to throw away a whole portion of our lives together.

....

Packing up and storing certain
painful memories helps me gain the courage
I need to face my future.

Both the wife and her husband knew their marriage had ended. They had tried, really tried, with marriage counseling and even personal therapy. They truly wanted to make it but couldn't.

Surprisingly, the dissension came not from the couple themselves but from their parents. Their parents had become dear friends and they adored each other's children as if they were their own.

Making the parents understand that they could still be friends, still have a relationship with their son-in-law or daughter-in-law, helped somewhat. Time proved that they could and, finally, they no longer chastised their children for a marriage that did not succeed.

. . . .

*Keeping a relationship with my
in-laws has been very important and I have
worked daily toward that goal.*

Gone Forever

Probably one of the most difficult situations is when the father or mother of our children disappears completely after the dissolution, and never has another thing to do with the children.

The children have enough burden to carry, for divorce is never easy on them, regardless of their ages. Some component of guilt is always present after divorce. They may fantasize about their missing parent, building up wild stories to help with their pain. "My dad's an ambassador in Portugal." "My mother is a CIA agent."

In the long haul, perhaps with professional help and with a great deal of love from the remaining parent, they will hopefully adjust to the other parent's desertion — never understanding but adjusting anyway.

. . . .

*I will recognize and help
my child deal with the vacant place
left by the missing parent.*

Except in unusual circumstances, there are winners and losers in every divorce. Losers can be construed in many ways, such as the one who was left behind or the one who had fewer assets.

Unfortunately, the loser is most often the one who thinks in terms of being a loser. It is awfully hard to get out of the victim mindset.

Rather than considering oneself a loser, it would be more fruitful to find ways to become the winner. This may require changing jobs, moving, making new friends and beginning new hobbies.

. . . .

As long as my marriage is over,
I can use this opportunity to make
the best of my new life.

It came out of the blue — totally out of the blue. Helen sat down to dinner one evening and announced to her husband of 47 years, "Herb, I went to see a lawyer today. I'm getting a divorce."

Needless to say, Herb was stunned, never having had a clue his wife was feeling discontented. She then left the table, packed up and drove away. He sat motionless in front of his cold dinner, too shocked even to cry.

As weeks rolled into months, Herb hadn't even begun his adjustment. He sat motionless much of the time. Now retired, he had few outside interests and didn't know how to reach out for help. Like many older men, he was having a terrible time dealing with his sudden divorce.

Those of us who have been hurt by sudden divorce can reach out to help others in similar situations.

Married young, divorced in their mid-40s, John and Sandra went their separate ways. Their children were grown so they no longer had to keep their marriage intact for the kids.

Many people "hang in there" until the children go to school or move away. With little animosity and often a great deal of affection for each other, they go their separate ways — each wishing the other well.

Rather then regretting the years spent together, so many people use the end of a marriage as a second chance to form new relationships, create exciting new lifestyles and make the rest of their lives the best of their lives.

....

With divorce I have the opportunity
to create exciting new
options for living.

Getting back into the stream of things socially, learning what it feels like to go on a date,
to be courted, to dance with another person
again, are some of the ways many of us use our
time after divorce.

Missing the companionship of being married, of having a best friend at home, very
often the newly single individual goes to social
functions actively looking for a new spouse.
Each person we meet is looked at as a potential mate.

When we don't give ourselves time to adjust
to being single, to learn what it feels like to be
alone, we may remarry too quickly. There are
multitudes of people also wanting to marry as
soon as possible.

. . . .

Realizing I married far too quickly,
I will put forth tremendous effort
to make this union work.

"Over and done with, and better that way," we tell ourselves. For a long time we stayed together just because it was too much trouble to end it. There wasn't anything horribly wrong in our marriage but not much was right either.

Getting on with adjusting to our divorce, we join clubs and generally try to keep ourselves busy. And it seems as though we are succeeding. Putting our ex out of our mind totally, we rarely even think about our failed marriage.

Then why do our dreams forsake us? Why, just when we feel comfortable about ourselves again, do we dream, over and over, about our lost love? It is a confusing situation, especially if we are already involved with another person.

. . . .

My subconscious helps me,
through dreaming, to deal with difficult
topics I refuse to think about
during the day.

AUGUST 23   *Losing Friends*

Rarely do the friends of a married couple who are divorcing stay friendly with both people. It would be far too difficult. Most often they feel alienated from either the husband or the wife.

Friends we have cared about and depended on for years will be lost. Old friends feel so comfortable and we mourn them as our whole social structure is undermined. No matter how hard we try, we may feel as though our social life will never be balanced again.

Establishing a new base of close friends may take years. It is hard work, learning all over again the give and take required of new friendships. Just as we work hard to settle into single life, we must also work hard to make new friends.

. . . .

Making new friends is hard work
but I intend to stick with it.

Usually one person is less than delighted about getting a divorce. Often it is the one who has more trouble making decisions and is frightened about learning to socialize as a single person.

Sadly, some people leave their marriages because another romance is already waiting in the wings. In surprising numbers, newly divorced people remarry within weeks of signing their final papers. The one who got left behind has a hard time making the adjustment to suddenly being alone.

Of the group of women who stay unmarried, health may begin to deteriorate. Physical problems such as headaches, ulcers and fatigue become more frequent and now they have another problem, poor health, to deal with as well.

. . . .

*It is more important now
than ever before for me to take
good care of myself.*

What a sad commentary on the state of our society today! So many of our young people are choosing to live together first, to see if they are compatible.

Afraid to commit to each other, many of these young people have lived through their parents' divorces. "We have to try it out first," they tell us, "to see if it will work." Interestingly, studies show there is a slightly higher divorce rate if the couple lived together first.

We have become so used to divorce, a term we rarely heard decades ago, that it is now an anticipated part of adult life. Half of us expect to fail. It is no wonder we do.

. . . .

I expect to succeed at my marriage.
I will be one of the 50
percent who do.

One issue we rarely think about when we are fighting still another battle behind closed doors is how our children will deal with our separation.

Naively, we tell ourselves that as long as we continue to give them food and shelter and enough money for clothing, they will do just fine. We forget that our children can also feel tremendous guilt at the failure of our marriage and will need far more from us than just having their basic needs met.

Kids need both their parents. Once their parents have separated, the children at least need to see them both frequently. Forgetting how needy our children are after the divorce will surely cause serious problems.

Even while I struggle to meet
my own needs, I must remember to
show love and support to
my children.

Raising a child as a single parent can, of course, be rewarding. However, shouldering the whole emotional burden alone can also be taxing.

This is especially true when the child feels terrible about the divorce and misses the other parent desperately. Additionally, there may be unnecessary guilt if in some way the child feels different from the other children in the family.

Perhaps the child has a learning disability, is handicapped or was adopted from another country. Feeling an extra burden on the parents, the child may either withdraw or unexpectedly act out. The single parent bears the whole brunt.

. . . .

I love all my children equally and
my being single doesn't
change that at all.

It is hard enough to suffer through the anxiety and stress caused by the ending of a marriage. It is worse when the sordid details become the topic of conversation in the community where we live.

They say the scorned partner is often the last to know. This may involve someone having an affair or getting involved in criminal activity. The embarrassment felt by the other person can be quite profound.

The sense of humiliation and rejection we feel, especially if we were wronged and we didn't know we were being "asked" indirectly for a divorce, is one of the most painful situations we will ever live through.

....

Holding my head up high,
knowing I have done nothing wrong,
gives me the strength to move forward.

Being Ostracized

It is common knowledge that over half of us divorce at least one time. There are many new circumstances we must become used to as newly single people.

Like early parenthood, which was so over-whelming, or the first few months on a new job, we now have to deal with brand new, often uncomfortable social situations.

One of the hardest realities, particularly for women, is realizing that old friends, especially couples, may ostracize us socially. Unfortunately, there is still the myth among married women that a single woman might try to steal their men away. We miss being with the people who used to make up our social structure.

. . . .

Since I can no longer be with
all my old friends, I will create a new
social circle for myself.

In the past, couples married very young, after high school or in their late teens. Nowadays, many wait until after vocational school or college to marry.

Moving from our parents' home where we often shared a room with siblings, to college — another shared room — to our marriage, where we shared yet another room, we were never autonomous adults.

Never having been on our own, budgeting, paying our own bills and dealing with problems as they arise, we are faced as newlyweds with more than just the task of adjusting to a new marriage. Awareness of the obstacles we must overcome should help pave the way for an easier adjustment.

. . . .

We will mature together,
so long as we both are willing to
contribute to the process.

Besides the obvious differences between males and females there are the curious ways we learn to deal with problems that are particularly stressful to us.

Some men know when their wives say, "I'll be ready in just a minute, honey!" that they can settle down and read the whole evening paper. Women, on the other hand, will never understand why some men would sooner drive 100 miles out of their way than lower themselves to ask a stranger for directions.

He doesn't remember to enter checks as he writes them; she never fills the gas tank. By accepting what we cannot change, we fully acknowledge each other's individuality. *Viva la difference!*

....

*I will accept patiently what
I cannot change.*

Depending on what our profession is, either husband or wife may need to get used to an alternative lifestyle. A husband who goes to sea for three months at a time or a wife who is a sales representative and is gone two weeks running, are both examples of this lifestyle.

Enduring long periods of separation from each other, we have learned to be totally independent, to handle parenting issues, to run the house, and to deal with stressful problems as they arise.

When the loved one comes home, we feel a certain sense of encroaching on our territory as they step in to share the responsibility. While our resentment is understandable, we must not let it rule our better judgment or we will undermine the very premise of being married.

. . . .

I must never forget that marriage
is a shared responsibility.

On Again, Off Again

It is a cycle we've all witnessed at one time or another: two people who love each other dearly just cannot get along with each other.

They fight continuously, decide they can't handle it and agree to separate. Over and over this behavior is repeated. Fight. Leave. Separate. Get together again.

Destined for divorce, yet still in love, they grasp at one last straw: to see a marriage therapist. It is hard work, this business of creating change, of learning to fight fair and express needs. They keep at it and, to our surprise and pleasure, they break the cycle.

. . . .

Old patterns can be broken if we are committed to each other and both want to change.

With summer over, school supplies are purchased, and new colored pencils and crayolas are packed into the traditional cigar box. The children are so excited.

During the first week of school, the second grade teacher has a short conference with each child to understand better any problems which may surface during the school year.

The teacher is amazed how few of the children shared the same last name as their mother. Our new norm, like it or not, is to anticipate divorce in over half of those who marry. This is a sad commentary on how poorly committed our society is to marriage today.

. . . .

Always optimistic, I will not allow myself to plan on divorce as part of my future.

The term "mixed marriage" brings with it all kinds of connotations, such as racial or religious differences. Rarely do we think of a mixed marriage as a blue collar/white collar situation.

These days we are not so bound by old social mores. We no longer limit our search for a spouse according to profession. What matters, we know now, is love, commitment and complete willingness to let each other be whoever they are — to work at whatever profession they wish.

She may be a waitress, he a lawyer. He may haul trash; she may be a physician. It is our common interests, our lifestyles and how we feel about one another that allow us to marry whomever we want.

. . . .

I married for love, to share our lives,
not to share our jobs.

The wedding was grand. A good time was had by all. If ever there were a match made in heaven, this was the one. Eleven years and two children later, for many reasons, the marriage ended. Bitterly. Nastily. The mother and children moved far away. Dad got visitation rights.

In this new society of ours — the one that accepts failure in marriage all too readily — the newly-divorced mom decided to cut the children off from their paternal grandparents. There was little they could do, legally or otherwise. Not only had they lost their daughter-in-law, whom they had adored, but their beloved grandchildren as well. It is sad that the children and their grandparents, who had important loving relationships, suffered so needlessly.

. . . .

My parents have a right to see their grandchildren and I will do everything in my power to assure that right.

The best of friends always, from the time they were very young, Tom and Althea realized that their relationship was no longer working. They hated to call it quits but they could see the handwriting on the wall.

Because they had three beautiful children, from six to 13, they wanted to make careful plans. Their separation was going to be awfully hard on the kids and they wanted to cushion the blow a little bit.

Carefully, they made plans, from financial to sharing custody, to their decision for one parent to be in the house two weeks each month, while the other went to the apartment they maintained. It is never easy but their thoughtful planning made a traumatic situation a bit less stressful for the children.

. . . .

Divorce is hard enough.
I can plan ahead for my children
and I can cushion the blow.

Sometimes we get into a mind-set of just not being good to ourselves. This is especially true if we have just undergone the breakup of our marriage.

For some reason, we tend to blame ourselves for a larger share of the problems than we may have actually caused. Feeling bad and guilty about what happened, it is easy to get into a cycle of not being good to ourselves.

It is time to learn to say yes to our own needs, to be good to ourselves, to do those things which make us feel validated and important. From taking hot bubble baths to doing volunteer work, saying yes will help us feel valuable once again.

. . . .

I am important and I do matter.

There is no time when we behave better with a member of the opposite sex than when we are courting each other. Best foot forward, demonstrating perfect manners, each of us tries our best to impress the other, as well as their family members.

For a short time after the wedding, this behavior may continue, breaking down only gradually over the months. To say we are surprised when our "perfect" spouse demonstrates less than perfect behavior would be an understatement. And then we need to decide if we are going to do anything about it.

Truly, there are only two choices. If we can live with the negative behavior, perhaps having a heart-to-heart talk about it, that is fine. If we find it too repulsive, harmful or unhealthy, most of us will sadly make the decision to leave. We now understand that courting is different from marriage.

. . . .

I no longer need to allow damaging
behavior toward myself.

No matter how independent we feel, a certain amount of dependence — of intertwining, of being part of a twosome — occurs during a long-standing relationship. Things are different after a divorce, even if we don't want to admit it.

Men and women alike say emphatically, "I took care of myself before I was married, and I can take care of myself now." We feel certain we can do just that.

What we forget is that we must take care of all the components of our lives. Telling our mothers that we are eating and sleeping well just isn't enough. Physical exercise, regaining our sense of self-esteem and becoming aware, once again, that we must fill our spiritual wells show that we really care about our own well-being.

. . . .

Even unmarried, I can take care
of all my own needs.

Feeling diminished by divorce, there are many of us who feel we have lost our whole social standing, our whole way of life, now that the relationship we depended on for so long has ended.

After all, we may have participated in a couples' bowling league, couples' bridge night and couples' gourmet club. Obviously, we no longer feel comfortable doing those things. Like trying to grasp mercury, trying to recapture what has slipped through our fingers is not possible. Compelled to marry again right away to become part of the couples set once again, too many of us rush right into second marriages.

We need time to be alone after divorce, to grieve and set about creating our new lifestyle. Readiness for a new love in our lives takes time, sometimes even years. We just can't rush the adjustment process.

*I want to marry again
but I must first give myself time
to be ready for a new relationship.*

Settling into his easy chair to watch the ball game, Paul felt a strong sense of contentment. Nothing was demanding his time and attention but the television screen.

Paul's marriage had been a mistake from the very beginning. He didn't know about his ex-wife's emotional instability until after the ring was on her finger. Later she became an alcoholic as well but Paul stuck with her for years, trying to help her get better.

Finally, Paul realized that he needed to change the focus to himself, to his own needs. He couldn't change a person who didn't want to change. Vowing never to marry again, Paul turned his attention to the game.

. . . .

*I am happy alone. I do not need
to be married to be valid.*

After the break-up, during separation but before our actual divorce, we are likely to feel lost, angry and hurt. What we didn't expect, however, is how the anger can overtake us.

Vicious thoughts may pop into our head, so we try to squelch them immediately. It is difficult to believe the things we may find ourselves thinking privately about our estranged partner. Not surprisingly, if we push away these thoughts during the day, we are more likely to dream about them at night.

It is perfectly okay to feel anything we need to feel, to think whatever thoughts we need to think, so long as we don't say them out loud to hurt another person. Getting it out of our system privately will allow us to move on to the actual divorce without needing to act out our negative thoughts.

. . . .

What I think is a private matter.
But I am responsible for how
I act out those thoughts.

The thought of keeping a journal is enough to frighten lots of people. We don't know where or how to start and may not ever have written anything before.

Sitting down with a notebook and a pen in hand, we should just let our thoughts begin to stream out. Write about a happy or bad time. Chronology doesn't matter; spelling doesn't count. What does matter is letting ourselves spew out our feelings — our anger, our lost hope and our lost love. We should write whatever we want to write.

It is amazing how cathartic writing down feelings can be. No one need ever see our journal and it won't be graded. Just doing it, day after day, will be helpful to our own emotional recovery.

. . . .

By letting out my pent-up feelings, I am moving toward personal contentment.

Equality and sharing seem to be the buzz-words these days. Women are liberated; men share chores and child-rearing.

In a recent societal turnaround, we find many well-educated women who have chosen to raise the children and run their homes as their current profession.

If it is financially feasible for only the father to work away from home, then the woman alone must make the decision, based on their needs, not society's demands. Making the mom feel *less than* women who work away from home makes no sense. Mothering and home-making are more than full-time jobs and are among the most noble of professions.

. . . .

Proudly we provide a strong, traditional, two-parent home for our family.

Yet another fight. Again yelled at for no reason at all. He never quite hit her but he raised his arm and threatened to do so all the time. Fearful, she never knew when he would erupt.

One evening, during an outburst, he screamed, "If you think you can do better than me, go ahead and leave. I can find a better woman than you any day."

With sudden clarity, his wife thought, "I don't need to live like this. I don't care anymore and I am leaving." That night she packed up and walked away.

No one should be abused. We all have the right to make choices and there are plenty of people who are willing to help us and support our decision.

. . . .

I will never allow myself to be abused again.

Children are usually very frightened when their parents divorce. They will often do everything in their power to prevent it, to hold on to the only security they have ever known.

In a surprising turn-about, some children, especially older teens and young adults, sit down with their parents to convince them that divorce may be their only answer. After the initial shock of being counseled by their children, some parents actually listen to what the children are saying.

There is no sense in staying together when a relationship brings only heartache and discontent. Many have stayed because of their children and are relieved by the "permission" to divorce.

. . . .

*I became courageous only after
my children gave me permission to
leave my troubled marriage.*

Several situations come to mind when we talk about "staying together under any circumstances." All of them are disastrous.

One story is told of the wife who developed a serious chronic illness. Her husband was quite frank about his feelings. She looked awful, he told her, and now she wasn't even capable of doing any of the fun stuff they used to do together. He would stay anyway because he was obligated to. This story has many variations; they all sound the same.

No one wants a person they love to stay bound to them because of pity. Pity destroys esteem. Having a spouse who hangs around, unhappily, feeling no love at all, is demoralizing and degrading. It is better to live alone than to be pitied.

. . . .

*Showing empathy and genuine compassion
are the only ways a well person can
stay with a sick spouse.*

Making love to one another is usually a wonderful and warm component of a life spent together. Comfortable as an old shoe, our two bodies fit together as one. Making love becomes an important way we express our love for each other.

When did lovemaking become a weapon instead of a pleasure? Sex used to be an absolutely joyful part of marriage. Now we may find ourselves withholding it as our relationship fails in other areas as well.

The choice between words as weapons and lovemaking as a weapon — is questionable. We can get professional help when various facets of our relationship break down. We can work together to save our failing marriage as long as we still love each other and want to stay together.

. . . .

We care too much to let our love go.
We are getting help because
we want to stay together.

Their family and friends were completely shocked. Nate and Minnie had the best marriage in their whole social group. When they announced their breakup, no one could understand why.

Keeping private matters private, Nate and Minnie went their separate ways. Or tried to. Every now and then they had dinner together, just to catch up on the news. Each time they had more fun together. One evening over coffee, they began to talk about why they had divorced.

The upshot of it all is that after two years of courting and individual therapy, Minnie and Nate remarried. Two people, understanding now their failure at marriage, became a wonderful success story. Years later, they are still happy.

. . . .

The end does not always mean the end.
It might just be the beginning.

It happens quietly at first. We sense something is wrong but we don't know what. We wonder if we have done anything to hurt our partner but we are told, "No, it's just that I am not happy anymore."

Finally, we begin to understand that our marriage is at risk. There can be many reasons for this to occur. We may have just grown apart over the years. One person may feel smothered by the other's personality or perhaps it is the sense that we no longer run like a well-oiled machine. There is friction all the time.

Deciding what to do can be paralyzing. Fear of being alone, of leaving the person we still truly love, can make us immobile. We have to make some kind of move, to a marriage counselor, rabbi or minister to help ourselves. Being unsure is too unsettling.

. . . .

I am frightened to leave my marriage but I am strong and I will survive.

Prenuptial agreements are a charged issue these days. We can't pick up the paper without finding another famous couple fighting about theirs.

It feels callous to be asked to sign an agreement when we are about to marry the love of our life. But we do have to keep in mind, even if we feel certain it won't be us, that 50 percent of all people who marry these days do get a divorce.

It is a highly individual and personal choice. If it is necessary to sign such a prenuptial agreement, then we must not let our love keep us from using good judgment. Getting a lawyer, our own lawyer, no matter how much in love we are, demonstrates our maturity and our ability to take care of ourselves.

. . . .

I will not let love cloud my ability
to take care of my own needs.

Sometimes it takes a good kick in the pants for us to realize what is going on in our lives which often takes the form of divorce.

Now alone, many of us find ourselves analyzing who we are and how we want to live the rest of our lives. Most importantly, whether we ever get married again or not, we still have to live with ourselves. By analyzing the person we have become, we can either stay the same or make some positive changes.

Wise people take the time after divorce to get in touch with themselves. People who were couch potatoes join gyms and exercise regularly. Others turn to their house of worship or go back to school. Divorce can provide a wonderful incentive to create change.

. . . .

Because I care about myself, I will strive
to become as healthy as possible —
spiritually, emotionally and physically.

One of the most troublesome problems for friends to deal with when someone they care about is having marital difficulties is to be asked to take sides. It is an uncomfortable and unfair situation for them to place us in, especially if our loyalties really lie with their spouse.

Faced with a disintegrating marriage, the distressed partners may throw propriety to the wind and try to give us details we don't really want to know. It is a difficult situation for all parties.

We can offer solace, we can offer sympathy but to offer our homes and our complete loyalty may be asking for trouble. Unfortunately, people who are divorcing can't depend solely on their friends. They must dig deeply and find their own inner strength as well.

. . . .

In the long run, despite help from my friends, I must depend upon myself for strength.

Even Mark and Jessie were surprised at how well their marriage was going. They both had wonderful jobs and lived a happy life together.

Mark was offered a promotion and they accepted, even though they were sad to move away from home since they were expecting a baby. Shortly after the baby was born, Jessie went back to work part-time. She was overwhelmed with work, a new baby, a new community and few friends. Their relationship became quite strained as she needed more from Mark emotionally than he could possibly give.

People can only take so much pressure, then buckle under the strain. Making demands that are heavy and unrealistic on the person we love is a sure-fire way to cause them to leave.

. . . .

It takes a long while to adjust to new situations. Rushing the process won't help us at all.

There are many different ways a relationship can end. How the marriage worked is often indicative of how it will end. Couples who talked out their problems will rationally talk over their separation.

There are those, however, who will feel so hurt by the ending of their marriage that they will use every verbal weapon in the book. Unfortunately, this often includes bringing up old fights and old wounds, and resurrecting them to fire at each other.

This type of breakup may also include such immature actions as cutting up the family photo album or breaking a favorite recording. Rarely physically abusive, the couple still feels an intense need to attack each other on an emotional level.

. . . .

Even though my spouse has become
emotionally abusive, I know I have made
the right move by ending our marriage.

She knows it is inevitable. Their marriage is done, and she has just sat down with him and told him so. She is completely shocked at his response.

Her husband, the man who has been Mr. Macho all these years breaks down and sobs. "I don't want it to be over. I'll change, really I will. I can't live without you." And he launches a campaign to stay married.

Flowers arrive at the door several times a week. He buys her chocolates and gifts. And he tries to overwhelm her with his caring. Too little, too late. Pretending to care didn't make up for all the years he didn't show her any attention at all.

. . . .

I have made my decision and I care too much for my own well-being to accept his tardy gestures.

Guilt is the feeling we have when we think we have done something wrong. Guilt will haunt us all our lives unless we actively deal with why we feel guilty.

We can place huge amounts of guilt upon ourselves when we are the one who has decided that it is time to end our marriage. Worried about backlash from our loved one, our parents and friends, and from our God, we feel the burden of guilt get especially heavy with the decision to divorce. This is, after all, not the way it was supposed to happen.

We may be overwhelmed with guilt at secrets we've kept, or with the memory that the person we married was really never our first choice, that we settled for second best. What matters most, guilty feelings or not, is that we do what is best for ourselves.

I know that first I need to leave my marriage. Later I will deal with why I feel guilty.

Each couple has a certain way of interacting. This behavior may have developed during the courting period or may have become finely honed after years of being married.

All of us know how to push their buttons when we are peeved with the people we love. Unfortunately, it seems we only do button-pushing when we are angry and looking for a fight.

There are positive buttons we can learn to push as well. This can become a habit, too — a wonderful habit. Taking the time to praise and listening to what our loved one has to say without judging are positive ways to do our button-pushing.

. . . .

I can learn positive behaviors easily. Now I am going to unlearn my negative ones.

For a long while we may have been happy in a strong and functional marriage. Then something changes. It doesn't matter what but we know that our marriage is over.

Overcome with sadness, the person who wants to stay married, who isn't ready to give up, may become quite vicious, verbally attacking the leaving spouse with every emotional weapon available.

There comes a time when we must accept the inevitable. It is up to us to decide whether we will accept it graciously or ungraciously. Bowing out graciously leaves our self-esteem intact.

My marriage will still be over but I can decide how to behave as it ends.

One of the hardest circumstances to deal with in a relationship is when one of the partners suffers from clinical depression. We can reach our hearts out trying to help but all we can really do is listen and love. No matter what we do, we can't make it stop.

Clinical depression must be treated professionally. Trying to lift the spirits of a depressed person, by telling jokes and making them feel happy, just won't work. Depression needs to be treated.

When the person we love is suicidal, we can only offer to make an appointment for help or, if they are willing, get them to a hospital. No matter how much we are in love with them, the depressed person has to want to get help and be open to therapy and, perhaps, medicine.

I cannot be on guard 24 hours a day. I must take care of my own needs as well.

We all know the rhyme "Sugar and spice, and everything nice. That's what little girls are made of." Sweetness and light. Smiling, skipping, jumping rope. The boys were a different story. They got to punch out their anger; it was totally accepted behavior.

As women, we have been taught to swallow our bad feelings ever since we were youngsters. Always squelching our anger, we were allowed to feel it but never to show it. It has now been proven medically that bottling up our feelings can make us physically ill.

We can learn to express anger and do so in socially acceptable ways. Alone, we can pound pillows and scream all we want. With others, we must learn to talk about our feelings and deal with whatever problems we cause.

I have a right to feel angry — and an even greater right to show it.

There will be many times in our lives when we will feel angry. Ending a marriage is bound to bring out anger — anger at our choice of spouse, anger that it is over and especially anger at how we may have been treated during our relationship.

One person told me he got in the car and went out to the country. There, all alone with the cows in the pasture, he screamed until he had no more voice. And then he sobbed and sobbed. Someone else mentioned how she threw marshmallows at the wall, ripping into bag after bag until she calmed down. Other people use physical exercise to vent their anger.

What matters now is that we deal with the anger we are feeling for all the reasons our marriage failed. If we don't, it is a sure bet we will carry that anger into our next relationship.

I am capable of expressing my anger. I give myself permission to do just that.

Many of us refuse to leave our marriages because we are afraid of living alone. We don't yet realize that it may be easier to live alone than to stay with a person who lives in the same house but pays no attention to us at all — never even answering when we speak.

There is a big difference between being alone and being lonely. Choosing to be lonely is a personal choice, when we deny ourselves friends to do things with, support groups and the many ways to become involved with other people.

When living alone we become especially attentive to the creaks and groans in our house or apartment — noises we never noticed before. Eventually we feel comfortable living by ourselves and the creaks and groans become familiar friends.

. . . .

I can depend on my inner strength to
help me adjust to being alone.

Interdependency, which is very different from co-dependency, occurs naturally in every marriage. Two people living together, who love each other, develop their own ways of mutually depending upon one another. To solve problems. For strength. For finances. And especially for physical affection. It's okay to lean on the one we love, as long as they are allowed to lean on us as well.

Handling problems ourselves, now that we are divorced, may seem a bit alien at first. It's most difficult not to pick up the phone and call the person you depended on for so many years to help you solve the problem. Dealing with single parenthood, not having enough money and just being lonely are all quite hard. We struggle to keep our own counsel.

. . . .

I tapped into my inner strength and
resolve often in those first months;
I am learning to stand alone.

What a surprise it is! No matter how badly we wanted out of our relationship, no matter how many problems we encountered living together, we are shocked at the rush of emotions we feel on the actual day we sign the final divorce papers.

Not expecting to feel anything but relief, we find ourselves wondering again if we made the right decision. Was there some way we could have kept it together — something we didn't do that we should have done?

Chastising ourselves serves no purpose. Other than reminding ourselves that we did, indeed, want this divorce and that signing the papers was quite emotional, we should feel proud that we have stood by our decision. It's okay to mourn a lost love.

. . . .

What is done is done.
I can now move on with my life.

Lawrence was irritable all day and he knew one of those headaches was coming. His co-workers asked him if he was all right; he was not the kind of person who snapped at others for no reason at all.

Finally, after work, Lawrence and his friend Solly went out for dinner. Over their meal, Solly said, "What's going on, Larry? I know something's wrong." Solemnly, Larry confessed that his ex-wife was getting married that evening and he felt strange about it. He told Solly he didn't love her at all anymore and didn't understand why it was bothering him.

The second marriage of a person we once loved dearly hurts us. The pure finality of it strikes home. We know our love has ended but this is the day we finally realize our ex will do fine without us.

. . . .

Today is the day I must finally accept that there are no more second chances.

It was getting more difficult for the couple to have a decent conversation. They both knew their relationship was in trouble but they weren't sure why.

One thing this couple knew is that they loved each other very much and both still felt committed to their marriage. They also knew they were growing apart. Together they sat down and talked about their options. Did they want to split up? No way. The love they felt was evident. And so they worked out a plan.

Carefully, over a period of many days, this loving and committed couple began to negotiate changes in their marriage. She gave a little; he did too. Compromise, telling the truth, changing patterns of behavior and knowing they loved each other saved their relationship.

. . . .

Our commitment to one another
is so strong that we are both willing
to change to stay together.

It was at a singles dance, the first one she had gone to since her husband split. Left. Walked out with no warning. She had gone intending to have a good time. Instead, she found herself shying away from any advance by a man. For more than two years after the divorce she refused to go to any singles event again. She didn't want to get involved, she told her worried and questioning friends.

We want desperately to keep ourselves from being hurt again. Our fear of being hurt may keep us from ever becoming involved in another serious relationship. Subconsciously, we may even choose people to date we know we would never marry. That way we stay protected from being hurt again.

. . . .

Until I rid myself of fear, I cannot
date seriously. I know now
I need professional help.

Listening without really hearing is a skill we all seem to have mastered. "Look at me, Mommy! I'm talking to you!" is the plaintive cry of children.

We pretend to pay attention but our mind is on a dozen other things — opening the mail, getting the messages off the answering machine — anything but looking at the person who is talking. This is one way our marriages break down. We just don't give full attention to the person who is speaking.

Learning active listening skills is not difficult. Look at the one who is talking and rephrase their words, reflectively but without judgment. For example, "You get angry when your boss yells at you." This opens the doors of communication and also tells the speaker we really care. Try it. You'll like the results it brings.

....

I can actively listen to the person
who is speaking and show I really care
about what they have to say.

People who are getting divorced often revert to childlike behavior. They feel emotionally needy and want us to know about it. It's no wonder they complain, for the very underpinnings of their lives have been torn apart and they don't have an anchor anymore.

By not knowing where to turn, or not having the stability of a marriage partner to come home to, the pattern of their days seems to disintegrate.

Now we understand why friends and family and the unconditional love and support they offer are so important. We won't stay needy forever. It's nice to know our family will love us no matter what happens.

. . . .

I know that when I feel needy there are people who will always love me.

The situation is not dissimilar to that of the woman on the delivery table, bearing down during final labor and yelling, "I'll never, ever, have another child!" Often she forgets the pain and has another child.

In the months after our divorce, we feel deep pain as well. We tend to remember only the bad things, the most hurtful memories. In fact, we may dwell on those thoughts to justify our decision.

Time passes and good memories begin to surface. Fun times. Happy moments. It's at this juncture we begin to doubt our original decision to divorce, to forget the pain we endured so often. This is a natural occurrence, a selective type of "good-memory amnesia," and it's time to remind ourselves that our choice to leave was fully justified.

. . . .

I took good care of myself when I made my decision to leave and I am still taking care.

Making one of the hardest decisions in our lives, to leave a person we at one time promised to live with all our days, can put us in a very emotional and fragile state of mind.

The one thing many of us need most is for our loved ones to validate our decision. Right or wrong isn't the issue here, it's in showing they care that affirms our right to choose. If a person we are close to acts negatively or angrily toward us, it can make us feel awful.

Each one of us knows when we can no longer stay in a relationship but it's both helpful and supportive to feel validated by our family.

....

I stand firm with my decision which is made easier with the support of loved ones.

Most of us remember the special feeling of being "best friends" when we were young. We played together, shared secrets and rattled on about boy and girlfriends. It was a special time.

As we matured and moved away from home, our "best friends" changed according to what we were doing at the time. Schools, jobs and frequent moves necessitated making new friends. Time passed and many of us fell in love.

What we never realized as children was that the person we would fall in love with and sub-sequently marry would also become our best friend — closer than any of our childhood friends ever were.

. . . .

We understand each other's strengths and weaknesses, faults and insecurities. Because we share so much love, we will continue to intertwine our lives together.

If, after confiding our divorce to a close
friend, the response is "I'm sorry. This must be
hard for you," we feel understood and vindicated. If, on the other hand, a friend snaps, "Well,
what took you so long?" we immediately feel
hurt and disappointed.

Why, we wonder, if they knew all this time
our marriage was in trouble, didn't they take
the time to talk to us about it? Perhaps, we
reason, our problems could have been worked
out if only we had known ahead of time what
they were.

This, of course, is not rational reasoning, as
we really would not expect our friends to offer
solutions to save our marriage. But most of us
would confess to harboring similar thoughts.

*No one can save a marriage but
the two people involved.*

At first it was only an occasional beer. Just one, on the way home from work. We didn't worry about it because we, too, had a social drink once in a while. One beer became several, along with chasers. Before we even realized it, the person we were married to had become an alcoholic. This was bad enough but then came the arrests for driving while intoxicated.

We did everything in our power to keep our spouse from drinking, and especially from driving while drunk but it didn't work. The inevitable happened: someone was badly injured in an accident caused by our drunk spouse. Now that the truth was evident, we decided we could not stay in our marriage and condone this dangerous and self-destructive behavior.

. . . .

I will not longer struggle
to protect my loved one from harm
or I as well will self-destruct.

Family rituals are so important. Sitting down at the dinner table together at least a few times a week is really important. Kids need continuity after one parent has moved out. Teens pretend they don't care but we know differently.

When the house is empty, eating alone becomes a difficult issue. Many people lose or gain weight when they no longer have a meal schedule. Meals get skipped or eaten at inappropriate times — like midnight.

By eating nutritious food and well-balanced meals, we are nurturing more than just our bodies. We are saying, in effect, "I care about myself. I am worth good food. I am an okay person."

*Part of my own recovery is learning
to take care of myself.*

There are many marriages that are not made equal. It happens, sometimes, that one of the partners, usually because of their profession, gets all the glory. This can happen with politicians, actors, writers, ministers and many others.

What is the appropriate way for a non-attention-getting spouse to act? This is not something we bargained for. Do we sit idly by, reveling in the glory bestowed upon our loved one? Or do we complain that we are being ignored?

Some can handle sudden popularity and being in the public eye, others can't. The ones who can't handle the strain wind up separating and, ultimately, divorcing. It's too bad, for in this case, their love is often intact.

. . . .

My damaged ego could not allow me to handle the role of feeling unimportant.

We hear these stories all the time. A young couple falls in love and ultimately marries. A few years pass and they have children. Everything is cozy and nice.

Circumstances change in everyone's lives. Perhaps we accept a promotion or one of us decides to further our education. The change may be intellectual or perhaps physical, as in a large weight loss or by working out regularly. This we can understand and tolerate.

Gradually we realize that our spouse has undergone more than just a little change. An accompanying personality shift has occurred — we no longer recognize the sweet and gentle person we fell in love with. If we cannot or are unwilling to blend our old personality with their new one, it becomes obvious that our marriage will not last.

. . . .

I mourn the person I married yet cannot live with this new personality. I will be better off living alone.

291

Before Suzie and Conrad got married they talked about having children and both agreed that neither wanted any. Both of them were on a high-power track for success and children would only be in their way.

As they climbed higher and higher up the corporate ladder, they grew apart. Suzie decided that having a child might hold their marriage together and Conrad reluctantly agreed. It was a last-ditch effort and they both knew it. A bouncing baby boy was born — a divorce soon followed.

Regardless of profession or level of education, a couple should not conceive a child to save a failing relationship. A new baby will only complicate matters further.

. . . .

I understand now that having a baby
could not save our marriage. Now
I must learn to be a good parent.

Finding out that their parents are going to separate or divorce is terrifying to some children — no matter how old they are.

Children will do anything to keep their parents together, including illness and temper tantrums. It's amazing how creative they get before and during the separation. By acting out, the children are covering up the real issues.

Kids wonder how they will have their basic needs met if their parents are no longer together. Will you still love me? Who will drive me to practice? Will we have enough money for groceries and clothes? Children need constant reassurance at this time.

I can continually reassure my children that all their needs will be met and that I still love them dearly.

There are a lot of us who are insecure all our lives. Raised without a nurturing family who loved us in an unconditional way, we bring to our adult relationships all the insecurities of our childhood.

Not knowing how to love unconditionally, we tend to place limitations on our relationships with our spouses and our children. Fearing loss, we still take the plunge and say, "Go ahead. Leave if you think you can do better." Or, "I'm leaving. This is not how life is supposed to be."

Not until we learn to deal with our own limitations, to give love without expecting anything in return, and to let go of our childhood problems, will we be successful in our relationships and our marriages. Then we will become mature adults.

I understand now that I need help to break my old behavior patterns and I am willing.

"Tell your mother I'm hungry and would like dinner now." Innocently, the child carries the message. He is told, "Well, you tell your father if he wants to eat he knows where the kitchen is."

Placing the children in the middle of our arguments is a horrible thing for us to do as adults. The child, who loves both parents, is confused and made to feel uncomfortable. The parents smugly think they are fighting without having to talk to each other.

Children should never be used as instruments in our marriage squabbles. They have enough trouble dealing with the fact that we are sparring and they don't need to be the referees.

I am adult enough to conduct
my fights personally.

New apartments. Separate lives. Now we have to learn to live as a single person. This is easier said than done because for years we have been a twosome.

How do we begin? What do we want for ourselves? One way to begin is to learn to sit in an easy chair, close your eyes and visualize what you want for yourself. It sounds difficult, but it really can work.

For instance, "I want a life with less stress — maybe a job that doesn't cause me to have a headache every night." This is a thought on which we can take action. New jobs can be found, new lifestyles created. Nothing is impossible if we are willing to work for change.

. . . .

I can create change in my life, first by dreaming, then by acting on my dreams.

Some of us were raised never to show our anger. It was okay to have feelings but not to show them. Anger swallowed year after year is destined to become resentment. Resentment destroys relationships.

There isn't a human being alive who can live their entire life without being angry at someone or something. When we are angry we need to talk about it, hopefully with some sense of calm, but we still need to get it off our chests.

Once we learn to talk about rather than bury our feelings, we stand a much better chance of keeping our marriages alive and well. Dumping our pent-up anger allows us to make room for joy.

. . . .

Resentment is gone from my life now but it could have ended my relationship.

Thrown back into a single lifestyle by the failure of our marriage, we wonder what other people think of us and how we will ever get back to dating and making new friends. It's a constant worry.

If only we open our eyes and look around us a bit, we will be most pleasantly surprised by the number of wonderfully friendly people there are. There are many support groups for the newly divorced, as well as neighbors and friends who will help if we will let ourselves ask.

Basically, people are really nice. Almost everyone is willing to lend a hand to a new neighbor and there isn't anyone who has so many friends that they cannot make room for one more.

....

It took a failed relationship to open my eyes to the friendliness and helpfulness of the people who surround me.

It's an agonizing decision. Tears are shed by both husband and wife. Fighting stops and starts again. Promises are made. And one of us moves out. Temporarily.

There are often false starts before a real decision is made to split up. Promises of undying friendship, of always being there to emotionally support the other and even of financial assistance are all made with the best of intentions.

Back and forth. Seesaw. Move in and out. Until the inevitable is realized and the separation becomes legal. We leave hoping for the best but knowing in our hearts it's really over. We both feel so sad.

. . . .

I can only deal with one day at a time.
More than that frightens me.

It never does us any good to have regrets about the failure of our marriage. Working hard to develop a strong relationship and a good marriage, we did not intentionally plan on our love ending.

Too many people leave their marriages with regrets, with words left unsaid, with dreams left incomplete. One thing we can do, even though it feels strange, is to sit down and take a moment to say goodbye to the person we have loved all these years.

By letting ourselves, or even forcing ourselves, to say the word goodbye, to give a final hug, we put closure to our parting. Much later, we realize how important those final words were.

. . . .

The tears I shed when I said goodbye
paved the road for my new life.

The time of making the actual decision is really hard. Do we separate or not? Should we try marriage counseling or not? Would it be a last-ditch attempt to hold our marriage together?

We may plague our friends at this time, calling them constantly and asking for emotional support. We are uncertain about how to handle this new and unwelcome problem in our lives. Our days are fraught with the constant surfacing of our problem — to leave or not.

Friends can listen and offer love and caring but in the end we must make our own decision about what we want to do. We are responsible for our own lives.

*I wanted my friends to help me until
I realized that only I can make
up my own mind.*

There comes a time in every marriage when the flame begins to die down just a bit, when we settle down to our lives together and may even take each other for granted. It's at this time that any marriage could use a good strong dose of romanticism.

This could happen in one of several ways. One partner may surprise the other with flowers, a home-cooked gourmet meal complete with fine china and no children at home. It may be a moonlight walk along the beach or a hot-air balloon ride.

What matters is that when the flame of love needs a little fanning, we fan it with some romantic overtures. In this way, we remind our loved one, and ourselves as well, how special our relationship really is.

....

We love each other so much. I need to remind myself to show it more often.

Remember the old adage: "The family that prays together stays together"? Nowadays, all the members of the family are involved in different activities and we rarely sit down together even for a meal.

Now we need to add a new adage: "The family that plays together stays together." It is so important to spend time together as a family, when we are not criticizing our children or asking them if they did their chores.

A game of baseball, a trip to the zoo or a movie or playing a board game like Monopoly are good ways to play together. Even cooking as a family, so long as the activity is fun and promotes laughter, will help us stay connected as a family unit.

. . . .

When my children grow up and move away, I want them to take along many happy memories.

When we fell in love as young adults and got married, we visualized how our entire life together would be "peaches and cream." We would always have secret love words and we'd never, ever have a fight.

Of course, we realized as we got older that no one has such an idealistic marriage. We fell into the pattern of married life, loving each other and, all too often, taking each other for granted.

Remembering to say "I love you" and really meaning it, is one way to reinforce our love for one another. Assuming the person we have committed to for life knows we love them is not as good as saying the actual words — and saying them often.

. . . .

I will not only remember to say
"I love you" but I also recognize
that I need to hear it as well.

Contrary to what others may think, marriage is a four-letter word. The correct way to spell it is o-u-r-s. There is no other acceptable spelling.

When two people love each other and they have committed their lives together, they think in terms of *us* and *ours*. If the relationship undergoes a breakdown, we begin to think only in terms of *me* and *my*.

When that happens, when we think only of what our personal needs are without considering the needs of our family members, we have turned inward toward selfish thoughts which have no place in a successful marriage.

. . . .

*My needs caused my marriage to end.
I am struggling now to understand
why I became so selfish.*

When asked as a youngster what marriage was, we most likely responded, "It's when a woman and a man live together and have children." This was our simplistic view of married life.

In reality, as we find the right mate and fall in love, then decide to get married, we know that a truly strong marriage will supercede our childhood expectations. A sense of lifetime commitment, a willingness to place our partner's needs ahead of our own, and an acceptance of the good and bad times show how a mature adult embraces the concept of marriage.

Thinking in terms of our family unit, working for the good of those we love and learning to make our own needs at times subservient are all traits that will enhance a successful relationship.

. . . .

I never knew I could love
anyone more than I love myself.
I am so happy that I do.

It is sad but true that some people who are secretly planning to leave their marriages begin to plan months or even years before they actually leave.

We hear horror stories about joint bank accounts being secretly emptied by the spouse who is leaving, and about thousands of dollars being charged on joint charge cards.

One way to discourage this kind of behavior is for the husband and wife to have individual accounts and charge cards. It's extremely important for women to have their own line of credit anyway but when a marriage appears to be a bit shaky, it's imperative.

. . . .

By having individual accounts and charge cards, I protect myself against loss and still have good credit.

Signing prenuptial agreements has always been a bone of contention before people get married. Some ask to have them, others don't. In some cases, it may be absolutely necessary, for instance, when we are ready to enter a second marriage.

In many states the prenuptial agreement is more important than a will. There is more at stake here than our own personal needs when we have children.

Prenuptial agreements will provide for our children should we die. Insurance policies and personal property can be held in trust for our children. This is true even in community property states. If we divorce again or if we die, even though we don't want to think of either, planning ahead will protect our children's interests.

. . . .

By taking the time to sign a prenuptial agreement, I have protected the financial interests of my children.

Getting a divorce is upsetting enough. Many people these days try to do it themselves or work together through a divorce mediator. This works for some but in more complicated cases or when there's a lot at stake, each person should have their own lawyer.

Even though our loved one talks to us rationally and calmly, even though we'd like to get it all over quickly, we should not rush into signing the papers. If we hurry through our divorce settlement without fully understanding all the consequences, we have no one to blame but ourselves if it doesn't work out well.

Divorcing is hard enough all by itself. There is no reason why we should complicate matters simply because we want it to be over and done with.

. . . .

*I will hire my own counsel
to protect my rights.*

So many of us were taught by our parents or our grandparents, "Never go to bed angry." This has always been wonderful advice but these days we need to carry it one step further.

In every home there should be a neutral zone, an area of the house where no fighting is allowed. Some families make it the kitchen, so that mealtimes are always pleasurable. Many couples call the bed their neutral zone and all fighting has to be done before they get into bed at night.

Going to sleep with bitter and angry thoughts left unsaid guarantees a poor night's sleep and a rude awakening. It's far better to finish the argument before we get into bed.

By spending the time to complete an argument, even if it is painful, I can awaken to the promise of a fresh new start.

There is such a thing as too much togetherness. We all need to spend some time alone, even as married couples. The writer Kahlil Gibran reminds us we must have spaces in our togetherness.

Many couples find themselves with either too much or too little time to be together. Both need to be remedied. We all need to spend some time together without our children, to keep the embers of our marriage burning.

It's helpful to sit down and discuss ways to be together. This may mean joining a bowling league, a literary club, taking a dance class, spending time doing a jigsaw puzzle together or taking a joint bubble bath. What matters is that we continue to have fun together.

. . . .

I will not let myself get so serious
and goal-oriented that I
have no time for fun.

In every women's magazine on the news-
stand these days and in a few of the men's,
there are articles about couples and the act of
love. So much is made of foreplay, yet the most
important piece of information is left out of
most of the articles. Foreplay does not just occur right before the act of making love. It's a
constant part of a successful marriage.

Couples who care dearly about each other
perform a casual sort of foreplay constantly.
They take the time to give a gentle kiss, to
bring in the morning paper, to heat the coffee,
and to find ways all day that signify their special caring, all of which set the stage for their
special act of making love.

. . . .

*Showing that I care and saying so
enhances our special
times together.*

Finally, Joyce and Arvid had saved money enough to go on a cruise. They had never vacationed in all the years of their marriage. Not knowing what to expect, they were overwhelmed by the lush cruise ship and their fellow travelers.

Having saved and planned so long for this trip, both Joyce and Arvid were upset when they had more than one brief fight. Exhausted from making arrangements at home, doing their work ahead for their jobs and getting everything ready to leave, may people find that a vacation doesn't always measure up to their high hopes.

Fatigued and stressed from all their advance preparation, Joyce and Arvid weren't sure how to relax together. And neither knew to ask the other what they needed or wanted to do.

. . . .

Next time we will take smaller, shorter vacations together. We need to learn how to relax first.

Totally shocked, Verna looked at her husband and began to cry. "You want a divorce? You're in love with someone else? I didn't know you were unhappy." Unfortunately, our partner may have been planning the separation and we weren't aware that there was a problem.

When one partner leaves in what seems to be a sudden decision, extreme shock and depression can set in. It may take years to get over such complete rejection by the person we loved so dearly.

Time helps, therapy often does, too. Most important, however, is the realization that we did nothing wrong and that the decision was made with no consideration for our feelings.

. . . .

It took me a long time
to regain my self-worth. I know now
I did nothing to cause our divorce.

After years together we have developed fixed habits, certain ways we live together. Slowly, the flame of love simmers down to a cool ember.

Sometimes it's hard to remember just why we were so enthralled with this person in the first place. What was it that attracted us? Attitude? Personality? Clothing? If we want to save our marriage, if we want to re-light the flame, then we have to pay attention and act as though we care. Acting will soon turn to habit.

We may have to begin by forcing ourselves to say nice things about each other, until we begin to mean them sincerely. Compliments about clothing or actions, or spending time paying close attention to conversation all show that we are trying to fan the flame.

. . . .

We still love each other and will work
together to brighten up our lives.

There is a time in life when a young man or woman gets ready to settle down. Perhaps they are finished with school or have become established in a good job. The time seems right to look for a spouse.

Before too long we become aware that the search for the perfect wife or husband is fruitless. There is no such thing as the perfect mate. Opening our eyes to reality will allow us to begin a realistic search.

Each of us will make some compromises but they will be compromises we can live with. Perhaps he doesn't have a gorgeous physique but his personality is wonderful. Maybe she is petite and we were hoping for tall, but she's so warm and intelligent it's just fine.

. . . .

Life is a compromise.
I dearly love the person I have
chosen to marry.

Huge numbers of us will, at some time in our adult lives, find ourselves in second marriages. This isn't something we actually planned but we have now found a special person to love.

Problems abound in many second marriages when the husband or wife places the first spouse in high regard, placing their current spouse second. It takes time for all parties involved to get used to a second marriage.

One can't immediately break down old allegiances simply because there has been a divorce. It takes time to get used to being married again. Gradually, allegiance and devotion shift to the new spouse.

....

It has taken time for us to become
fully committed to each other.
I am glad we waited it out.

More and more these days we meet people in what we call blended families. His children, her children and perhaps even their children as well. All trying hard to become a unified family. And often having a hard time.

The problem with being a blended family is that not all the ingredients will always mix together well.

With time, compassion, patience, genuine love, persistence and gentleness, everyone in the blended family will work together to become one family unit.

. . . .

We tried and tried to become a family.
Happily our persistence paid off.

It begins with two people who fall in love. Standing together, the couple should have the right not to be interfered with. They have love on their side. And they really believe in one another.

Once they marry, assuming their love stays intact and grows as it should, little will come between them. They develop a sixth sense and a very deep trust in one another. When meddling in-laws enter the picture or old friends attempt to muddy the water, they still stand by one another, no matter who is trying to interfere with their lives together.

Trust is one of the most important components of a strong marriage — complete and total belief that what our spouse is telling us is true.

I absolutely believe my loved one,
now and forever.

Finally, our children have grown, got their own jobs and their own lives away from their childhood home. Then one of our adult children calls to ask if they can move back in, having divorced or having financial problems.

Many of us feel we have to say yes. After all, this is our child and that child is having personal problems. Little do we consider what will happen to our privacy when we allow our adult child to move back home. This is the time of life when we both expected and are entitled to be alone as a couple.

Rules will have to be set, about how long they can stay, about participation in the chores and perhaps about paying rent. No adult child should have a free ride. At least not for very long.

. . . .

For a short while we can help
our adult child with finances but then
we must consider our own needs.

It seems as though we have finally found the right person to marry. Although we hadn't really anticipated getting married again, true love has entered the scene and we can picture ourselves spending the rest of our lives with this wonderful, warm person.

There is, however, one fly in the ointment. Even though they admit to being in love, there are some people who just cannot commit to a long-term relationship. This may be especially true if there are children in the picture, which automatically frightens some people away.

Once we recognize that the person is not going to commit to getting married we have two choices. The first, of course, is to end the relationship. The second is to accept the limitation and stay unmarried but continue to see one another.

. . . .

*I have too much self-respect to
stay unmarried in this type of situation.
I will have to break it off.*

It is a threat many of us have heard before. The question is, do we really take it seriously? The relationship is soon to be ended. There is no saving it.

"If you leave me I'm going to commit suicide. I can't live without you!" This frightens us, since we care very much. Besides, it would be awful if we were put in a position of feeling guilty if the person ever really did it. Generally these are idle threats, made when they are hurt or disappointed.

Each of us needs to do what will make us the happiest and most secure. While we care deeply, it should not stop us from leaving a relationship.

I am not responsible for anyone else's behavior but my own.

The strong but silent type, Bart really loved his wife Linda, yet he had a hard time telling her. It was even harder telling her when he was angry or upset.

One day on a television talk show he heard someone say that some people find they can write in a letter the things they can't say in person. Then they can choose to use it either for catharsis or to give to the other person. The idea of writing out his thoughts really appealed to Bart.

Imagine Linda's surprise when she found his letter on her dressing table one morning. Bart rarely even gave her a card — he was a man of few words. In the letter, Bart was finally able to say how much he cared about her and what she meant to him. From then on, they used letters for something special or to talk about hurt or anger.

. . . .

It does not matter whether we
write or say the words; what matters
is that we say them.

Some of us like to be alone a lot. Others find it a punishment and are frightened to spend too much time by themselves.

We can conquer our loneliness by challenging ourselves to do something about it. When does it bother us most — after work, in the evenings, on weekends? By sitting down and making some phone calls, it's simple enough to make plans ahead with a friend, to join a class or to get tickets for an anticipated event.

We needn't be afraid of being alone. What we should be afraid of is our inability to do anything about it. Be creative. Loneliness can be conquered.

. . . .

I choose to make plans and
not to be lonely.

324

It would be hard to be part of a family without expecting that some of our best laid plans will become disasters. When they do, we must decide whether to get hysterical and angry or whether we can turn those dreadful times into future family memories.

Split pea soup was simmering in their brand-new pressure cooker. The family couldn't wait for dinner. Lots of ham in the soup, fresh bread and then . . . **kaboom!** The split pea soup had exploded in the kitchen, running down the walls forming stalactites on the ceiling.

Feeling lucky that no one was hurt, the whole family scurried around to clean up the remnants of their longed-for dinner. The children were silent, then dad began to laugh so hard he had to sit down. Soon they were all laughing. A real mess but a great story!

. . . .

*It is always my choice whether
to laugh or cry. Laughing
makes me feel better.*

Recently, a well-known comedian said on television that he may never have children, since
he was quite sure he would compete with them
for attention. He gave examples but they all
boiled down to our need as adults to succeed,
to do it better than anyone else.

It's fine to make that decision ahead of time
but once we have the children, we really do
need to make a conscious decision to let them
be children and let them have the limelight. We
are, after all, not their equals. As their parents
we need to act adult — most of the time.

Giving praise to a child for a good somer-
sault, a fine painting or good behavior only
enhances our success as parents.

. . . .

Even though I am tempted,
I know I must not compete for
attention with my children.

Wonderful qualities make us a unique couple or family. It's not just the *way* we all act toward one another but the special things we do, the things we make and *how* we all act toward one another.

From the quilt Great-grandma made of patches from a generation's worth of our old good clothes to Dad's special barbeque sauce, to Mom's homeknit sweaters, to Grandpa's twinkly eyes and warm hugs, we carry in our mind's eyes history of our uniqueness.

Encouraging the unique qualities in us all, as a couple and as individuals, allows the very best in each and every one of us to surface and to shine. And it creates fun times and wonderful memories.

I cherish and savor all those
individual qualities that create
my unique family.

Charlene and Jon always enjoyed going out with their friends for dinner, especially when they tried one of the new gourmet restaurants.

Pulling back her chair, Jon inquired if Charlene felt comfortable. He was so solicitous toward her, the epitome of a gentleman. All her friends were envious of his chivalrous behavior. Charlene knew better, for in the privacy of their home, Jon was quite different — rude and often abusive.

Knowing better than to say anything in public, she was always hurt and confused by his quick change to being nasty at home. Charlene accepted his two-faced behavior as her lot in life. She reasoned, "My husband treats me better than my father treated Mom, so I guess I can live with it." Each person has to decide.

....

*Until I am unwilling to accept this
type of behavior, I know
it will continue.*

One thing was certain, Mandy and Truman loved each other and they had been deeply committed all the years of their marriage. Their life together was good.

Truman knew he was a good provider and considered himself a good husband and father, too. So did Mandy. But there was a problem. Now that the children weren't around so much, Mandy wanted Truman to talk to her more — it was too quiet now.

They were operating on completely different wavelengths. Truman was sure he was doing all he needed to do to be a good husband and provider. Mandy knew that but needed a little more from him. She needed conversational give-and-take, and finally she asked for it.

. . . .

Once I learn to be specific about
my needs, I then can expect an
appropriate response.

Each time they had a fight it was worse than the time before. In the first years of their marriage, it was fun to make a joke of it to family and friends. "Oh well," Jenny would explain, "you know how much fun it is to make up!" Indeed, most people who have been in love remember those early making-up years.

Brian kept up the fighting, however. Years passed, and Jenny struggled to hold on to her love and to a marriage that was actually making her ill. The children became so upset each time their parents fought that they began to cry.

Jenny realized making up was no fun — in fact they almost never did. Their marriage was just not good. Finally, Jenny began to value herself and wanted to protect her children. Her only choice was to end the marriage.

. . . .

I value myself enough to leave.
Now I can look to the future for my
children and for myself.

Harriet liked all the members of Marcus' family. One by one she met them in the months they were dating, except for Ted who was in the Navy. Marcus' favorite brother Ted was the one he cared about most.

When Harriet finally met Ted, she and Marcus were already married. She despised him. He was rude and crude and far too . . . well, personal with her to make her feel comfortable. Then Marcus dropped the bombshell. Could Ted live with them while he looked for a job, maybe for a few months? Harriet was dumbfounded. Faced with one of her most difficult adult decisions but wanting desperately to please her husband, she reluctantly answered yes, provided they all sit down to talk about house rules and limitations of time.

I am pleased with my ability
to handle a difficult family situation.
I hope I did the right thing.

For a long time they wanted children but it never seemed to happen. They knew it was really a last-ditch effort anyway to save their marriage, so eventually Shirley and Donald divorced.

Six weeks after the divorce, nauseated and weak, Shirley saw her doctor. What timing! No husband and pregnant. Shirley had a decision to make. Should they get together again or would she go it alone?

After much soul-searching, Shirley realized that it wouldn't be right to re-marry Donald just for the baby. Her happiness mattered too so he would have to be a father without living in the same home.

. . . .

I am a responsible adult and I
have faith in my ability as
a single mother.

Sitting down with her mother at lunch, Pearlie burst into tears. "What's wrong, honey?" her mother wanted to know. "Jerry only pays attention to John, Jr.," she cried. "It's as if the girls don't exist."

This situation is not at all uncommon when one parent, for some reason, picks a favorite and virtually ignores their other children. If the parent won't listen to reason and won't get some help with this problem, there is little we can do except try to balance out the problem a bit by giving extra attention to the ignored children.

Pleading for understanding won't work and neither will talking to the favored child. Something in that parent's background is pushing to favor only one child.

. . . .

*Understanding my spouse's childhood
problems can help me keep things
balanced with our children.*

We always say that time heals all wounds but that old adage may not always hold true when it comes to children whose parents have gone through a divorce.

Even though we try to smooth the way for our youngsters to make the transition as easy as possible, our efforts may not be enough. They always secretly hope that their parents will get back together. The new marriage of one parent may be enough to throw the child into depression. So may a move to a new school.

Only professional therapy will help with depression. No amount of boosting spirits or trying to make the child happy will help. Time does not always heal the wounds.

. . . .

I understand that depression is
a disease. I will no longer blame myself
for another's depression triggered
by my divorce.

A most peculiar thing happens when divorce occurs. People we were friendly with continue to see the male half of the divorced couple but often find themselves uncomfortable with the woman if she is alone.

Women can decide that this is their fate and that they will have to drop old friends who are still married. Yet there are so many creative ways we can see our old friends. Perhaps the ladies can go out for lunch or to see a show. Or invite them over with other people, a mixed group of married and unmarried couples.

The point is that we don't have to give up our married friends if we don't want to. It may take some creativity and perseverance, but it can be done.

. . . .

In spite of the difficulties and logistics involved, I will work to keep my old friends.

The child really took a bad fall. The bicycle skidded on gravel near their driveway. Knees and elbows bleeding, she ran home crying. After her father cleaned her up and gave her a hug, he told her, "These things take time to heal."

When she broke up with her college beau, she called home crying on the phone. Her daddy reassured her once again: "These things take time to heal, honey. Give it time, sweetie. You'll be okay."

When her marriage ended, she didn't need to call on her father. Instead, like most of us, she reached deep into her personal resources. "This will take time," she thought. "I need to let myself heal."

. . . .

The breakup of my marriage doesn't
mean that I am not a worthy person.
I have self-worth, and I will give
myself the gift of time.

So much had changed since the early days of their first love. Twenty-four years had gone by and with them many changes had occurred.

Both husband and wife were working full time jobs now, as many of us do. Edward was feeling tired and depressed much of the time but couldn't figure out why. "Get yourself some therapy," coaxed his wife.

"I can't," he said. "I'm afraid it will be too painful for me." Edward knew he had issues from childhood that had lain dormant for years and that the time had come to face his problem. He was scared.

Making the first move, saying we need help, is a good beginning. Then begin to see a counselor. Therapy is not easy but it almost always helps.

. . . .

***By learning to trust the therapist and myself,
I opened up and began to heal.***

Sammy remembered when he was small, and his Grandpa died. He burst into laughter when he was told. Without hesitation, his dad slapped him across the face. "People do not giggle when something sad happens. You are a bad boy for laughing at such a sad time."

Sammy always remembered that warning and learned, as most of us do, to control his emotions in a more appropriate fashion. Then his long-term relationship with his fiancee fell apart. Shaken and very sad, Sammy found himself in the uncomfortable position of feeling like laughing whenever anyone asked him what had happened.

He sought therapy and found out that he was not bad, nor were his actions inappropriate, he just needed to learn how to handle his feelings better.

. . . .

Laughter and tears are closely related, and I have the right to my own feelings.

Chrissy always wanted to learn ballroom dancing but her husband Mike would never agree to go along. She would have felt uncomfortable going by herself so she just let it drop.

One day it occurred to Chrissy that since they were no longer married, she could do anything she wanted to do! She didn't need permission and she didn't need Mike to take the lessons. The experience was glorious. Chrissy not only learned to ballroom dance but she enjoyed it so much she joined a club and continued after her lessons were over. New friends, a new skill and a new club, all from her newly found freedom and independence.

....

*I have given myself permission
to participate in life.*

When going through sales training for a new job, some trainees are taught to act as if they expect to get the sale, as if they are the most confident of salespeople.

The "as if" method can work for those of us who are struggling to get back into the dating picture. If we act as if we feel comfortable with ourselves and what we do, these will soon become our real feelings. If we act as if we are proud of our accomplishments, soon we will be.

Pretending is okay as long as we can measure up to our own pretense. Shy people can become less shy. Unhappy people less unhappy, all because of "as if."

. . . .

Acting as if I am happy and confident has helped me become that way permanently.

Depressed by our current state of affairs, unattached and feeling unwanted, we may make some personal decisions we'll regret later on.

One of these may be changing jobs and moving to get away from all the bad memories. Unfortunately, we take all of our memories with us wherever we go. By moving, we have left behind all our familiar stomping grounds, our entire support team of family and friends and a job we may have enjoyed. If we are the custodial parent, we will deprive our children of their other parent as well.

Decisions made in the heat of hurt feelings may be decisions we will regret for years. After divorce, we need to give ourselves at least a year before we make any major decisions at all.

By forcing myself to stay put, I avoided what would have been a terrible decision.

When someone dies, we remember them for a long time as they really were, flaws and all. As time begins to pass, we start to build a pedestal to put them on, to make them perfect.

This is also very common when a divorce has occurred. Somehow with the passage of time, we tend to forget all the reasons why we left the marriage: the fighting, the money arguments, the communication problems. We tend to idealize our ex-spouse as we think back over our marriage.

We must remember the bad stuff, too. If we make that person perfect in our minds, we will blame ourselves for leaving such a perfect mate.

. . . .

I was right to get out of an unhappy marriage. I need to remind myself often that it really was unhappy.

Once in a while, rather than feeling any sense of relief once the dissolution has been finalized, we feel lost and afraid, clinging to the hope that we'll get together again, afraid of making it alone. Confusion reigns.

With any relationship, from puppy love right up to the real thing, if we are so overwhelmed with feelings of love and devotion that we can't even consider living without that person, then what we are dealing with is not just love, but insecurity, too. Certainly after the divorce we may feel more unsettled than ever.

Recognizing that we can live without the person we were married to, that we are worthwhile and important, will help us move away from loss and into acceptance of our new position in life.

. . . .

If I ever fall in love again, I can still maintain my own identity.

Those of us who are unmarried parents all face the problems of dealing with our children when we decide to date again. From getting responsible sitters to having children act up when we leave, it can all become overwhelming.

One situation we never anticipated, however, is our child really becoming attached to someone we are ready to break up with or don't like in a serious way. For a while we find ourselves tempted to keep up the relationship because our children are begging us to.

Once we realize how foolish it is to continue dating a person we are not serious about just to please our children, we can move on to make our own decisions, based on our own needs.

. . . .

Although I love my children, only I will decide whom I want to continue dating.

In today's society many people choose to marry for a second time. Because we've been married previously, there are likely to be children to consider. In fact, both people may be bringing children into the marriage.

It's important to discuss ahead of time each other's views on how to raise the children, how to discipline and other problems. If a spouse's views are completely disparate, we really may be headed for some difficult times, especially with teenagers.

Each party will have to compromise as no two people raise their children the same way. What matters most is that each supports the other's decisions and that their general viewpoints are similar.

....

It is not easy to be a step-parent but since we support each other in child rearing, we'll do fine together.

Bad news travels fast. Of course, we hear all the awful stories that happen to people who place personal ads in the newspapers.

Rarely do we hear about the good ones, the encounters that are highly successful. Cherry and Roger met through an ad she placed. When he responded to her box number, Cherry was very careful about not giving him her last name or telling him where she lived. They met in a local restaurant for coffee and hit it off very well. Not until several coffee dates later did she invite him to her apartment.

A good friendship developed and looked as if it was leading to something serious. Cherry followed all the good sense rules. Not all dates from personals work out and there is risk, so each of us must decide what to do.

. . . .

Placing a personal ad was hard
and one of the bravest things
I have ever done for myself.

We may not even recognize that we are doing it until a good friend points it out to us: "Do you know that you are comparing everyone you date to your ex?"

It had been our intention to be really open to the dating game, to change our frame of reference to allow different types of experience. Yet many of us find ourselves trying to "replace" our lost spouse — even if there was no love lost between us at the end.

This is a strange subconscious thing we do and it indicates that we are not yet over the disappointment of our severed relationship.

. . . .

By understanding what my needs are, I can be open to all types of new relationships.

For over 20 years Perry and Audrey had been close friends. They met in drama class during college and had stayed friends all these years.

Perry was recently divorced and was spending a great deal of time with Audrey. Before too long, they were dating. As it often does, the question of intimacy eventually came up. Thinking it over a long while, Audrey told Perry, "If we become intimate after all these years and then we stop dating, our friendship will end. We need to decide if we can handle that if it happens."

Not all people would make the same decision but they decided their friendship was too valuable to risk. In some cases, it's easier to find a new marriage partner than to replace a longtime friend.

....

Not becoming intimate was a difficult decision but one I was strong enough to make.

Grandfather did it all the time. His children and grandchildren tolerated his behavior, but when they saw it happening in their own families, that was a different story. Now they wanted to get rid of this abuse.

Home from work, he'd greet his wife with a kiss and "Hiya, ugly. Go to the dog pound for that new hairdo?" His verbal abuse, covered in poor humor, was hurtful and embarrassing to the whole family. No one was exempt from his smiling barbs and half the time they couldn't tell whether he was being mean or nice.

The person who never shows anger or gets physically abusive just doesn't see themselves as being abusive. Only we can decide if we can live with it or not.

· · · · · · · · · · · · · · · · ·

I am a good person and do not deserve to be abused. I will not tolerate it any longer.

There is an unspoken rule for divorced parents: "Never speak badly of your ex-spouse in front of the children." There is a lot we'd like to say, since we have bottled up many of our bitter feelings. But, poisoning the children against their other parent serves no purpose except to deprive them of someone else they love. Rather than feeling vindicated, we will eventually wind up feeling guilty.

After all, we are the adult in the house and should never treat our children as confidants, regardless of how old they are.

. . . .

The temptation is great to speak harsh words
but my brain over-rules my heart.

For so long we have lived with another adult, a person whom we loved and who would always be there if there should be an emergency.

As a single person, we are the only ones responsible for what happens to us. There is no excuse not to have emergency numbers by the phone, or candles and matches ready for "lights out." We need to have a doctor who knows us and our medical history, close friends available if we feel ill and well-thought-out contingency plans for other situations.

Living alone does not mean we should not be responsible and not be ready to handle situations we would have taken care of together as a married couple.

. . . .

If I am prepared for emergencies,
I can then rest well.

The sun glistened on the new snow — a cold, wintery day. We remember how the snow crunched underfoot as we used to go together to choose our Christmas tree.

This year is different. Shopping alone for a tree, we know it will be decorated with only half the ornaments we collected so lovingly all those years. The other half went to our ex-spouse.

We have begun to create new personal memories, new rituals of our own. From collecting special new ornaments to sharing the evening with our friends or family, we understand that with or without a partner, we can enjoy our new holiday traditions.

. . . .

Any decision I make about how I celebrate holidays is an okay decision.

Sometimes couples who love each other but are not communicating well, try one of the Marriage Encounter groups that are available in many areas.

This may seem like grasping at straws, since these marriages may already be headed for divorce. Instead, it may be an opportunity to fix what is wrong, so long as there is caring and commitment underneath it all. Couples learn to show love, to listen to each other, to talk about needs and to reaffirm their love.

Smart couples do something for their ailing marriages before they break down. Marriage Encounter, counseling, going on a religious retreat or seeing a minister or rabbi may all help.

*All relationships need
maintenance and repair.*

Years ago the program *Saturday Night Live* had a character called "Wendy Whiner." She spoke in a whining voice and annoyed everyone around her.

Occasionally, when someone we know is going through bad times in their marriage and perhaps trying to decide what to do, they become either "Walter" or "Wendy Whiner." It's hard for us to deal with, since our friends are acting like spoiled children.

Certainly we all want to be there when the people we love are having any type of problem. Acting childish, whining and having emotional temper tantrums drive away even the most steadfast of friends.

. . . .

From today forward I am through
with childlike behavior.

One of the hardest adjustments to make after we are separated or even divorced is that we have few social plans and little determination to make any.

For those of us who have largely depended upon being with our spouse and our "couple" friends, our social life falls apart. If it matters, if we want to be with friends, then we will need to become our own social director. Other people like to make plans, too, and many will be happy that we thought to invite them. Considering exciting new options like canoeing, a new restaurant or a short vacation can be great fun.

We have to determine our own needs and take care of them by ourselves. No one is going to do it for us.

By planning ahead I can fill my own needs for activity and be with friends as well.

It wasn't until after all the children were gone
and they were nearing retirement age that Greg
and Carin felt they were taking each other for
granted, that there wasn't any excitement left at
all in their lives.

Confused, and even a bit frightened, they
went to a marriage counselor. They learned that
what was happening to them was normal at
their stage of marriage, and that they could put
the spark back if they wanted to. By remembering what they used to love about each other, by
doing special little things together, they were
able to resurrect their old commitment. They
even joined a stamp collecting club and began
to square dance again.

. . . .

My life is only boring when I allow it to be.

There are right and wrong times to bring up serious issues. Some people are masters at the art of poor timing, spurting out their feelings "whenever."

In any long-term relationship there will be smoother places and periods when the road is a bit more bumpy. When the potholes begin to form, it's important to talk about our problems — but not at an inappropriate moment. When the new mom is nursing her baby, it is not a good time to talk about financial trouble. When Dad is under the car changing the oil, it is not a good time to talk about teenagers and discipline.

By choosing our time carefully to talk about our troubles, we guarantee the full attention of the person who matters most to us.

. . . .

*By discussing our problems
as they occur — at the right time,
we stay on a smooth road.*

Even if we are relieved it's over, even if there was no way the marriage could have survived any longer, it is still hard to get used to life without a husband or wife.

The wise person will give themselves all the time needed to get used to being single. There is no way to hurry adjustment, to grieve more quickly than we are able to for our loss or to become comfortable with making all our own decisions and not having to consult anyone else when we make plans.

It takes time to restore the sense of order in our lives, to feel comfortable with ourselves, with how we live and with the patterns we establish.

. . . .

I grant myself all the time I need
to adjust to being single.

Promises are made when we are young and in love that can be very difficult to honor later in life. Truly, we mean to keep them but it doesn't work out.

One of these situations is the issue of religious differences. "Honestly," we say, "it doesn't matter which religion we use when raising the children" — and we mean it. However, when Communion or Bar Mitzvah time comes about, when going to Sunday school and learning about the basic tenets of our religion matter, we may tend to forget our sincerely-made promise.

Both husband and wife need to decide, preferably ahead of time, how to raise their children. For the sake of continuity and to develop religious beliefs, children need to know where they stand.

. . . .

By deciding ahead of time, we will
provide our children with a
a good religious education.

As younger people, we feel immune to all the problems and pressures that adulthood can bring. Little do we understand the real problems that are ahead.

When a serious difficulty occurs, like a chronic illness, a severely handicapped child or the loss of a job, some people just cannot handle the pressure. What they do instead is pretend the problem doesn't exist at all. By refusing to talk about it, one partner completely closes out the concerns of the other.

Problems don't go away when we refuse to talk about them. Instead, they grow and multiply until it is nearly impossible to deal with them at all.

I will try to find some way to communicate successfully with my partner.

Promises made in the heat of passion don't always carry through to the cold light of morning. It isn't that we don't intend to keep our word but it does often happen that we don't.

Unfortunately, too many individuals use this type of promise to keep us on the hook, so to speak, manipulating us emotionally. Eventually we get tired of being promised something only to be dangled just enough to keep us believing.

It takes two people to create this marital manipulation — one to make the promise and the other to keep believing it will come true.

. . . .

I will no longer delude myself with unkept promises. This only keeps me from trusting my loved one.

None of us consciously wants to be abused in any way, physically or emotionally. If we are, we may think we will just give it back twice as hard.

Underneath all the game playing, most couples really do love each other. Still, they might be acting like children because they don't know any other way to behave. It is not unlike what we used to do in the schoolyard when we called out, "Nanny, nanny, boo boo." Instead of sticking out our tongues at each other, we fling harsh words back and forth.

We are not children any longer. One bad word does not deserve another. Unless we stop playing the game, we may wind up with no partner to play with at all.

. . . .

From now on I will not rise to the bait of verbal abuse. I respect myself too much to participate anymore.

It's a quiet kind of punishment that most of us will recognize from our family or someone we know.

He goes to play cards with the guys, she decides to leave his dishes in the sink and not wash his clothes when she does a family load. She goes to the mall; he forgets to do the grocery shopping or to put the roast in the oven for dinner.

This is childish behavior. We're unhappy about what our spouse is doing but we don't have the communication skills or the courage to talk about it. So we quietly punish. Not only is this behavior totally fruitless but it sets a bad example for our children.

. . . .

If I am angry I will say so. Playing games takes too much energy and serves no purpose at all.

It's one thing to have a fight with someone we love and to forgive and forget. It is another to have a fight and not forgive ourselves for doing the fighting.

This kind of behavior can lead to guilt and to shame. Continuing to blame ourselves for having a fight serves no purpose except to lower our already rock-bottom self-esteem. All couples fight. It is a natural way to express emotions. Almost all couples make up. That is another natural way to express emotion.

By not forgiving ourselves, we hold onto guilt that may ultimately fester, grow and ruin the very relationship we cherish.

I believe I am good and I believe in my Higher Power. Together we will work to heal my need for guilt.

Times Square. Watching the ball drop as we got ready to sing "Auld Lang Syne." These are New Year's Eve memories from our past, spent with a person we truly loved.

Now New Year's Eve has arrived again. Friends have tried to coax us out of the house. "Come to the party with us. You'll have a great time!" But it's okay not to go and it's even all right to "dwell in the house of our own misery."

In order to heal we need to grieve. To grieve, we need the passage of time. Feeling sad and lonely is fine — it is normal — and we will begin to feel better soon.

. . . .

I give myself the gift of time for this new year, to think of old memories and to separate myself from my marriage.

Best Sellers From HCI

ISBN	TITLE	PRICE
0-932194-15-X	Adult Children of Alcoholics	$6.95
0-932194-54-0	Bradshaw On: The Family	$9.95
0-932194-26-5	Choicemaking	$9.95
0-932194-21-4	Co-Dependency	$6.95
0-932194-61-3	Following The Yellow Brick Road	$9.95
0-932194-40-0	Healing The Child Within	$8.95
0-932194-39-7	Learning To Love Yourself	$7.95
0-932194-25-7	Struggle For Intimacy	$6.95
0-932194-68-0	Twelve Steps To Self-Parenting For Adult Children	$7.95

Orders must be prepaid by check, money order, MasterCard or Visa. Purchase orders from agencies accepted (attach P.O. documentation) for billing. Net 30 days.

Minimum shipping/handling — $1.25 for orders less than $25. For orders over $25, add 5% of total for shipping and handling. Florida residents add 6% sales tax.

Health Communications, Inc.
Enterprise Center, 3201 S.W. 15th Street
Deerfield Beach, FL 33442-8190
(800) 851-9100

More Affirmation Books

DAILY AFFIRMATIONS: For Adult Children of Alcoholics
Rokelle Lerner

Affirmations are positive, powerful statements that will change the ways we think, feel and behave. *Daily Affirmations* has also been recorded on audiocassette, where author Lerner is joined by Dr. Joseph Cruse.

ISBN 0-932194-27-3 .... $ 6.95

Set of Six 90-Minute Tapes
ISBN 0-932194-49-4 .... $39.95

SAY YES TO LIFE: Daily Meditations for Recovery
Leo Booth

Say Yes To Life takes you through the year day by day looking for answers and sometimes discovering that there are none. Father Leo tells us, "For the recovering compulsive person God is too important to miss — may you find Him now."

ISBN 0-932194-46-X .... $ 6.95

TIME FOR JOY
Ruth Fishel

With delightful illustrations by Bonny Lowell, Ruth Fishel takes you gently through the year, affirming that wherever you are today is perfect and now is the *TIME FOR JOY!*

ISBN 0-932194-82-6 .... $6.95